The Chicago Diner Cookbook

Chef Jo A. Kaucher

Book Publishing Company
Summertown, Tennessee

Front cover design and photo: Warren Jefferson
Back cover photo: Mickey Hornick
Interior design: John Wincek
Photography: Olympic Photo, Conscious Choice/E. Kugler

Published in the United States by
Book Publishing Company
P.O. Box 99
Summertown, TN 38483
1-888-260-8458
www.bookpubco.com

Printed in Canada

ISBN-13 978-1-57067-136-4
ISBN-10 1-57067-136-2

14 13 12 11 10   11 10 9 8 7

Kaucher, Jo A., 1952-
  The Chicago Diner cookbook / by Jo A. Kaucher.
      p. cm.
ISBN 1-57067-136-2
1. Vegetarian cookery. 2. Chicago Diner. I. Title.
TX837 .K2598 2002
641.5'636--dc21

2002012538

The Chicago Diner
3411 N. Halsted
Chicago IL 60657
773-935-6696
773-935 VEGY (8349) fax
www.veggiediner.com
chicagodiner@sbcglobal.net

Book Publishing Co. is a member of Green Press Initiative. We chose to print this title on paper with 100% postconsumer recycled content and processed chlorine free, which saved the following natural resources:

BOOK
PUBLISHING
COMPANY

24 trees
669 lbs of solid waste
11,024 gallons of water
2,289 lbs of greenhouse gases
8 million BTU

green
press
INITIATIVE

For more information visit: www.greenpressinitiative.org. Savings calculations from the Environmental Defense Paper Calculator at www.edf.org/papercalculator

Table of Contents

Acknowledgements

I would like to thank the following...

My mother, sister, and grandma, who instilled a sense of taste and adventure in me with great recipes and experimenting in our home;

To the seitan king, Oscar Gonzales, for his energy and the many years of vegetarian cooking experience he shared with me at the Diner;

To all the regulars who have supported us—it is like cooking for a big family...a variety of meals at different times...daily coming back for more;

To our restaurant staff...over the 20 years...it is been a medley of creative, interesting people...with the day-to-day hard work and challenges;

To my friends in the Chicago natural foods community;

To Marsha and Hans...for helping us open the Diner with naiveté and dreams and many days and nights of cooking, cleaning, talking, arguing and laughing;

A deep thank you to Lara...for her hours of typing and listening and helping organize the years of Diner recipes;

To Cynthia and Bob...for their energy and persistence in making this book a reality;

A special thanks to my loving friend and partner Mickey...a memory of "I will find you wherever you are and we will open a restaurant." Thank you for the support and guidance, and most of all, the humor;

And to all cooks, chefs, interns...for over 30 years I have been cooking and serving natural foods and appreciating the joy of cooking without meat.

Love animals, don't cook them.

Introduction

In the early 1970s, Chicago still had an image as hog butcher to the world because of the infamous stockyards that inspired Upton Sinclair's muckraking novel, *The Jungle*. But change was in the air; the stockyards closed for good in 1971, and people were starting to seek out vegetarianism as part of an alternative lifestyle. Chicago Diner chef Jo Kaucher was working as a baker in a nonprofit natural foods store (she's mentioned in Studs Terkel's 1974 classic *Working*) when she stopped eating meat on a dare. But as she learned about animal rights and the health and environmental dangers associated with eating meat, she decided to stick with her new diet.

A few years later, Mickey Hornick, a former Chicago commodities trader, was driving a limo and looking for something more meaningful to do. He saw a "Dishwasher Wanted" sign in the window of his favorite veggie hippie haunt. He decided to apply for the job at the Breadshop Kitchen, even though the owner said she was getting ready to close the place.

The Wrigleyville cafe stayed open for another year, mostly due to Mickey's blood, sweat, and tears—and those of cook Jo Kaucher, as well.

While working at the cafe as a jack-of-all-trades, Mickey met Jo and fell in love with her light, tasty vegetarian creations—a rarity in those days of heavy, bricklike veggie fare. They eventually went their separate ways—Jo to California, and Mickey seeking new horizons. But when the restaurant finally closed in 1981, Mickey decided to take on the lease. "I was looking for a place where people treated each other with respect—for a capitalistic business with a high moral code.... We haven't always succeeded, but we have tried our best."

The first thing he did was recruit Jo, who was back in town. Due to inexperience and lack of funds, the pair—who became partners in life as well as business—took nearly a year of hard work to open the new place.

Mickey and Jo

Lunchtime would roll around, and Jo, an avid experimenter, would take a look into the refrigerator. One day she found a pound of tofu, a green pepper, a red pepper, a baked potato, and an onion. They had only one cast-iron skillet, so she started slicing, dicing and sautéing—and the ever-popular Home-Fry Deluxe was born.

Jo's relationship with food dates back to her first job: selling popcorn at a movie theater while growing up in Chicago's northwest suburbs. The self-taught chef also worked at a grocery store deli counter, tended bar, and waitressed before getting behind the line at a handful of restaurants and hotels. But she found it increasingly difficult to work in the world of meat and potatoes. "I'd pick up a big slab of meat and slice it and dice it and make big burgers out of it, and I'd think, 'Why am I doing this? I'm the vegetarian.' It was a reality check."

It was only natural that she would turn to whole foods cooking, and Jo's recipes come straight from the heart. "It's an intuitive process," she says. "When I see different ingredients, my mind kind of puts them together and I have a really good idea of what they taste like." For inspiration she's always consulted the most classic of recipe books, *The Joy of Cooking*—without the meat, of course—as well as *American Wholefoods Cuisine* by Nikki and David Goldbeck. "I always go back to the basics, and *Joy of Cooking* gives the basic outline of each dish. In my mind I always take away the meat, fish, and poultry and put in tofu, tempeh, or seitan and take out the white sugars and such." The result has been a menu full of healthy, tasty takes on American classics, such as the Diner's Mushroom Stroganoff and Vegan Lasagne.

THE CHICAGO DINER COOKBOOK

Before the Diner opened in 1983, German animal rights activist Hans Kostka signed on as comptroller and unofficial partner, and set up the accounting system on a Mac. Mickey didn't go vegetarian until opening day—and stuck to it partly because of Hans' impromptu lectures about "blood and bones" and animal rights (which would occasionally get on a customer's nerves).

The banks told them they'd never make it without serving chicken and fish. And then there was that ambiguous name—Chicago Diner. "The name didn't make sense to a lot of people," says Mickey. "We had some top advertising people tell us we were shooting ourselves in the foot by not telling people what's going on here. But we knew they would find us."

"The Diner is of the times," says Jo. But instead of hamburgers and meatloaf, customers can order Tempeh Sloppy Joes, a Radical Reuben, Groovy Gyros, Blue Corn Cakes, and Not Dogs—and most items can be made vegan as well as wheat-, sugar-, soy-, and yeast-free. Over the years, popular specials, such as the lentil and tempeh Shepherd's Pie, have been added to the menu, and Jo is always cooking up new takes on old favorites like the Tofu Scrambler Jubilee. (Mickey jokes that she tries out her experiments on the customers, whose suggestions have shaped the menu since the Diner opened.)

Jo doesn't always measure ingredients and generally cooks by instinct. She stretches out with catering, creating such items as Caponata with Crostini Rounds, Artichoke Salad, Mexican Bruschetta, Mini Polenta Cakes, and Pesto Pasta Spirals; for holidays there's Diner Kiev and Tofu Roulade. She was part of the only vegan team among 900 at the 1984 International Culinary Olympics, headed by top vegan chef Ron Pickarski. They won two silver medals. "I felt proud that we could show the world that vegetarian isn't weird, and that we'd won awards in a competition against the meat-eaters of the world," she says.

below: Culinary Olympics, 1984

Over the years the Diner has drawn regular folks and celebrities alike, from families who come in each and every Sunday to luminaries such as Madonna, the Red Hot Chili Peppers, John Astin, Boy George, Cloris Leachman, Smashing Pumpkins, Marilu Henner, Ellen Burstyn, Dave Matthews Band, Indigo Girls, Moby, Woody Harrelson, Kevin Bacon, John and Joan Cusack, and Roger Ebert—who gave a thumbs-up to the Diner a few years ago on *The Tonight Show* with Jay Leno (he's a fan of the Cocoa Mousse Cake). Afterward, the phone rang off the hook for days.

Selling veggie burgers and "not dogs" at street fairs has also helped bring in new customers. "They would see that we didn't have horns on our heads," said Mickey. A thriving gay neighborhood has grown up around the Diner, which now caters to walk-by traffic as well as hard-core vegetarians. Vegan Diner staples such as oat bars, muffins, cookies, scones, cakes, and dairy-free cheesecake are sold at the local Whole Foods Market. And for five years, Mickey and Jo ran a suburban branch of the Diner in tony Highland Park.

This collection of recipes goes back to the basics—the now-classic Diner items that customers have asked how to make again and again. They have come from imagination, experimentation, and the inspiration of cooks and others who've shared this food over the years.

"We're trying to cook food that's not just vegetarian, but also tasty," says Jo. "People always say they want to cook vegetarian but don't know where to start. We hope this cookbook helps. We want people to eat smart and live well. I raise my glass high in a toast to all of you. Enjoy."

— CARA JEPSEN

THE CHICAGO DINER COOKBOOK

Appetizers

Leslie's Mushroom Spread

Hummus

Baba Ghanouj

Grande Nachos

E-Z Artichoke Dip

Vegetable Quesadillas

Caponata

Polenta Rounds or Triangles

Olive Tapenade

Leslie's Mushroom Spread

3-4 SERVINGS   *Thanks, Leslie!*

½ cup	diced onion
1 tablespoon	olive oil, soy margarine, or butter
4 cups	coarsely chopped mushrooms
⅓ cup	chopped walnuts
¼ cup	white wine
¼ teaspoon	nutmeg
½ teaspoon	salt
pinch	pepper

In a medium skillet, sauté the onion in the oil until translucent. Add the mushrooms and walnuts and cook 2 to 3 minutes. Add the wine and spices, and simmer about 5 minutes. Pour into a blender or food processor, and pulse on and off quickly a few times. Pour into a serving dish and serve chilled with your favorite crackers and garnished with parsley.

Hummus

6 SERVINGS *Hummus tastes great served in a stuffed tomato or made into a pita pocket sandwich. Adding a piece of kombu to the beans while cooking helps eliminate gas from the beans and speeds up the cooking process.*

½ pound	dried garbanzo beans
2 quarts	water
½ cup	coarsely chopped green onion
½ cup	parsley
3 tablespoons	minced garlic
¾ cup	tahini
½ cup	lemon juice
1½ teaspoons	salt
¼ teaspoon	cayenne pepper
1 or 2 tablespoons	extra-virgin olive oil

Bring the beans and water to boil, and simmer 1½ hours or until they are very tender. (The softer they are, the creamier the hummus.) Drain the beans, reserving approximately 1 cup of the liquid.

Place the beans in a food processor with the reserved liquid and remaining ingredients, and process until smooth.

Variations:

☞ Fold roasted red pepper into the hummus purée.

☞ Sprinkle with chopped black olives.

☞ Use white beans or black beans.

☞ Substitute 2½ cups canned beans for the dried beans and water.

Baba Ghanouj

4-6 SERVINGS   *Call it eggplant caviar or dip. This appetizer goes great with vegetable sticks, pita bread, or crackers.*

2 or 3	medium eggplants
5 or 6 cloves	garlic, minced
¼ cup	lemon juice
⅓ cup	tahini
1 teaspoon	salt
2 teaspoons	ground cumin
2 tablespoons	chopped parsley

Preheat the oven to 425°F. Slice the tops off the eggplants and cut in half lengthwise. Place the sliced halves on an oiled baking sheet (cut side down), and bake approximately 30 to 45 minutes until the eggplants are soft and tender. Turn the halves over for the last 15 minutes, and add the minced garlic. To test for doneness, pierce with a fork. When cool, scoop out the pulp except for the seeds.

Place the cooled eggplant in a blender with the remaining ingredients, and mix until it reaches the desired consistency. Adjust seasonings to taste. Pour into a container and refrigerate until ready to serve.

Grande Nachos

8 SERVINGS

Everyone loves nachos—traditional crunchy tortilla chips, layered with your choice of fixin's.

2 quarts	water
1 pound	pinto beans
2	bay leaves
	Mexican spices to taste

NACHO FIXINGS:

1 (14-ounce) bag	tortilla chips
2 cups	chopped tomato
1 cup	sliced black olives
1 cup	chopped green onions
½ cup	minced jalapeño peppers
2 cups	shredded cheddar cheese
2 cups	guacamole
½ cup	Dairy-Free Sour Cream (p. 126)
2 cups	Quick Salsa (p. 76)

Bring the water to a boil in a large pot. Add beans and bay leaf. Return to a boil, cover, and simmer approximately 1½ hours or until tender. Drain, reserving some of the liquid. Blend the beans in a food processor, adding any reserved liquid needed to make a smooth dip. Add the spices, and adjust to taste. If a spicier taste is needed, add chopped jalapeños.

To make the nachos, create a mountain of tortilla chips and place a dollop of the bean dip onto each chip. Layer with fixings as desired.

E-Z Artichoke Dip

4-6 SERVINGS

This dip is sure to win over guests of all ages. Using eggless mayo helps reduce cholesterol.

1 (15-ounce) can	artichokes packed in water, drained and rinsed
½ cup	eggless mayonnaise
1 tablespoon	chopped fresh dill
1 clove	garlic, minced
½ pound	spinach, cooked and chopped (optional)
	salt and pepper to taste

Place the artichokes in a food processor, and blend until semi-smooth. Transfer to a bowl, and fold in the mayonnaise, chopped fresh dill, garlic, spinach (if using), and salt and pepper to taste.

Variation: To make this a hot dip or spread, add to the basic recipe:

1 cup	shredded mild, white cheese
2 tablespoons	Parmesan cheese
1 teaspoon	hot pepper flakes

Mix all the ingredients together, and place in shallow baking dish. Broil until brown and bubbly. Serve with pita chips, crostini rounds, or rye toast points.

Vegetable Quesadillas

A Mexican version of a grilled cheese sandwich. A quick, easy appetizer or a meal—and the sky's the limit on your favorite fillings.

FILLINGS:

2 cups	chopped spinach
¼ cup	chopped onion
½ cup	chopped mushrooms
OR:	
½ cup	chopped onion
½ cup	chopped peppers
¼ bunch	chopped cilantro
OR:	
½ cup	chopped broccoli
½ cup	chopped cauliflower
½ cup	chopped zucchini

6	corn or whole wheat tortillas
	oil for sautéing
	mild cheddar or other cheese, grated

TOPPINGS:

Quick Salsa (p. 76)
Dairy-Free Sour Cream (p. 126)
guacamole

Heat the oil in a sauté pan, and quickly sauté the filling 3 to 5 minutes. Set the filling aside.

Heat a large nonstick skillet or pan, or spray oil on an ordinary skillet. Place a tortilla in the pan and sprinkle with cheese and the vegetable filling mix. When the cheese begins to melt, fold the tortilla over in a half-moon shape.

Remove the tortilla, place on a cutting board, and cut into triangles. Serve with salsa, sour cream, and guacamole.

Caponata

This tasty Sicilian recipe is served as a salad, relish, or hot over pasta.

2 or 3 cloves	garlic, minced
1 pound	eggplant (2 large), peeled and diced
1 cup	diced onion
1 cup	diced red bell pepper
1 cup	diced green bell pepper
½ cup	chopped celery
3½ tablespoons	olive oil
1 cup	diced tomato
2 tablespoons	pine nuts or toasted sunflower seeds
2 tablespoons	raisins or currants
½ cup	chopped parsley
¼ to ⅓ cup	balsamic vinegar
1 tablespoon	salt
½ teaspoon	pepper

Sauté garlic, eggplant, onion, peppers, and celery in the olive oil in a large skillet over medium-high heat until tender. Add the tomato, pine nuts, raisins, parsley, vinegar, salt, and pepper. Serve chilled with warm crispy bread rounds.

Polenta Rounds or Triangles

6 SERVINGS
AS APPETIZER;
4-5 DINNER
SERVINGS

The base of this appetizer is the polenta, but it has a wide variety of toppings. Use your imagination and have fun!

3 cups	coarse cornmeal
9 cups	cold water
1 tablespoon	salt
½ cup	corn kernels
1 teaspoon	nutritional yeast
2 teaspoons	garlic powder
2 teaspoons	onion powder
½ teaspoon	pepper

Cook all the ingredients in a large saucepan over medium heat, stirring constantly to prevent burning. Cook and stir approximately 5 to 10 minutes, until it thickens. Cool. Pour into an oiled sheet pan. Use a cookie cutter to make rounds, or cut into squares. Top polenta with:

* Pizza sauce and melted cheese

* Sun-dried tomatoes and olives

* Pinto bean paste, avocado slices, and cilantro

* Sautéed spinach and garlic

Olive Tapenade

6-8 SERVINGS

This spread goes great on toasted crostini rounds, toast points, crackers, breads, etc.

½ cup	ripe black olives, pitted
½ cup	green olives
¼ cup	kalamata olives
½ cup	sun-dried tomatoes
¼ cup	chopped green onions
1 tablespoon	minced garlic
1 cup	soft tofu or ricotta cheese
drizzle	olive oil

Place all the ingredients, except the olive oil, in a food processor, and process until smooth. Slowly drizzle in a little olive oil if needed for a creamier consistency.

Breakfast & Breads

THE VEGETARIAN CHICAGO DINER

Lemon Poppyseed Muffins

Scones

Diner Hash

Dairy Pancakes

Buckwheat Pancakes

Blue Corn Cakes

Nut Milk French Toast

Biscuits

Home-Fry Potato Deluxe

Dairy-Free Quiche

Sausage Patties

Ex-Benedict

Brunch Burrito

Banana Poppyseed Bread

Diner Cornbread Muffins

Focaccia

Irish Soda Bread

Basic Wheat Bread

Fruit Preserves

Fruit Salsa

Lemon Poppyseed Muffins

10-12 SERVINGS *These are a moist, delicious summertime treat.*

1 cup	whole wheat pastry flour
1 cup	unbleached flour
⅓ cup	turbinado sugar
2 teaspoons	baking powder
½ teaspoon	baking soda
1½ teaspoons	poppy seeds
¼ teaspoon	salt
1 cup	soymilk
4 teaspoons	oil
¼ teaspoon	grated lemon zest
1 teaspoon	lemon juice

Preheat the oven to 375°F. Lightly oil the muffin pans. Mix the dry ingredients in a medium bowl. Add the soymilk, oil, lemon zest, and lemon juice, and stir until moist. Spoon the batter into the muffin pans, and bake 25 to 30 minutes.

Variation: Add 1 cup of fresh berries or chopped fruit to the batter.

Scones

An easy and tempting treat to entice your holiday guests. Serve scones with a little jam and a warm drink. Your friends will love the homemade delight!

1½ cups	unbleached flour
1½ cups	whole wheat pastry flour
4 teaspoons	baking powder
5 tablespoons	turbinado sugar
½ teaspoon	salt
1 teaspoon	cinnamon
8 tablespoons	soy margarine
½ cup	currants
1 cup	soymilk
1 tablespoon	lemon juice

Preheat the oven to 375°F.

In a large bowl mix the dry ingredients. With a pastry cutter, cut in the margarine until blended well. Add the currants. Make a well in the center of the dry mix, pour in the soymilk and lemon juice, and quickly mix by hand. The batter should be sticky. Pour it out onto a floured board or counter, and knead lightly 1 minute. Let the batter rest a few minutes, then roll out with a rolling pin to 1½-inch thickness. Cut with a cookie or biscuit cutter.

Bake for about 15 to 25 minutes, until firm and browned on bottom.

Diner Hash

4-6 servings

This dish is a Sunday brunch favorite with the regulars. It goes wonderfully with Scrambled Tofu (p. 94), Biscuits (p. 27), and Diner Gravy (p. 129).

8 ounces	tempeh, cubed
1 tablespoon	vegetable oil
2 teaspoons	tamari
2 tablespoons	oil
1 cup	diced onions
1 cup	diced bell pepper
4 to 6	baked potatoes, peeled and cubed
2 teaspoons	fennel seeds
½ tablespoon	oregano
pinch	dried red pepper flakes
½ teaspoon	salt
¼ teaspoon	pepper

Preheat the oven to 350°F. Toss the tempeh with the oil and tamari. Spread the tempeh on a cookie sheet, and bake for about 15 minutes.

In a large skillet, heat the oil. Add the onions and pepper, and cook until onions are translucent, about 5 minutes. Add the potatoes, herbs, and tempeh, and cook 2 to 3 minutes more. Adjust spices to taste.

Dairy Pancakes

8-12 SERVINGS

For a special treat, you can add fruit, nuts, or chocolate chips (kids love 'em) to the batter.

1 cup	whole wheat pastry flour
2 cups	unbleached flour
1 tablespoon	baking powder
1 tablespoon	baking soda
1 teaspoon	salt
3	eggs
⅔ cup	honey
2 cups	milk
1 cup	apple cider

Sift the dry ingredients in small bowl. In a separate bowl, mix the wet ingredients. Whisk the wet ingredients into the dry ingredients, and blend well.

Spoon the batter onto an oiled griddle or skillet. When bubbles appear on the top of the pancake, flip with a spatula. Brown the other side, and remove from the pan. Serve with warm maple syrup or fruit sauce.

Buckwheat Pancakes

6-8 THREE-INCH PANCAKES

These hearty pancakes will get you going and keep you going on cold winter days.

1 cup	unbleached flour
¼ cup	buckwheat flour
2 tablespoons	turbinado sugar
2 teaspoons	baking powder
¼ teaspoon	salt
⅛ teaspoon	cardamom
1¼ cups	vanilla soymilk
2 or 3 tablespoons	vegetable oil

Mix the dry ingredients in a small bowl. Slowly add the wet ingredients, and whisk until smooth.

Spoon the batter onto an oiled griddle or skillet. When bubbles appear on the top of the pancake, flip with a spatula. Brown the other side, and remove from the pan. Serve with warm maple syrup or fruit sauce.

Variation: Add fruit or nuts to the batter.

Blue Corn Cakes

8-10 SERVINGS

For a neat Fourth of July treat, put out some blue corn pancakes layered with a few traditional pancakes, and garnish with warm strawberry sauce and maple cream.

1½ cups	blue cornmeal
⅔ cup	pastry flour
⅔ cup	unbleached flour
¼ cup	rice, soy, or oat flour
½ teaspoon	baking soda
1 teaspoon	baking powder
pinch	salt
½ cup	vegetable oil
¼ cup	raw sugar or rice syrup
2¼ cups	soymilk

Mix the dry ingredients in a large bowl. In a separate bowl, mix the wet ingredients. Mix the dry ingredients into the wet ingredients; stir well.

Spoon the batter onto an oiled griddle or skillet. When bubbles appear on the top of the pancake, flip with a spatula. Brown the other side, and remove from the pan.

The mixture keeps refrigerated for a few days, or you can freeze the mixture. After thawing, you may need to thin it out a bit by adding in a little soymilk.

Variation: To serve these cakes as a dinner course, omit the sugar and add herbs of your choice. Serve with sautéed vegetables and top them off with your favorite sauce.

Nut Milk French Toast

2-3 SERVINGS

Experiment with breads—try using cinnamon raisin bread, a nutty bread, or thick-sliced Italian bread.

¼ cup	raw cashews, sunflower seeds, almonds, or walnuts
1⅔ cups	hot water
1 teaspoon	cinnamon
½ teaspoon	nutmeg
1 teaspoon	vanilla extract
pinch	salt
¼ cup	sweetener of your choice
2 tablespoons	oil
4 to 6	bread slices

Soak the nuts in hot water 15 minutes; drain. Blend the soaked nuts with the water, cinnamon, nutmeg, vanilla, salt, and sweetener in a blender until smooth. Pour the mixture into a shallow dish.

Heat the oil in a large skillet over medium heat. Dip the bread slices into the mixture, and cook each side until golden brown. Serve hot with maple syrup, applesauce, or your favorite fruit sauce.

Biscuits

ABOUT 18 BISCUITS

These warm and flaky biscuits can be served with our Diner Hash (p. 22), scrambled eggs or tofu, or by themselves with your favorite fruit preserves.

5 cups	unbleached flour
1½ tablespoons	baking powder
1 teaspoon	baking soda
½ teaspoon	salt
1½ sticks	soy margarine
2½ to 3 cups	soymilk
1 tablespoon	lemon juice or white vinegar

Preheat the oven to 425°F.

Mix together the three dry ingredients. Cut in the soy margarine until the mixture resembles peas. Combine the soymilk and lemon juice or vinegar, and stir into the dry ingredients until the flour clings together. Turn out onto a floured board or countertop, and knead 1 or 2 minutes until the dough is smooth. With a rolling pin, roll out the dough to ½-inch thickness, and cut with a cookie or biscuit cutter. Place on an ungreased cookie sheet, and bake 12 to 15 minutes.

Variation: Add your choice of herbs to the dry mix.

Home-Fry Potato Deluxe

2 SERVINGS

While opening our first restaurant, Mickey and I were hungry, but not all of our produce had arrived. So I gathered up what we did have available, and to our surprise, I created the HPD. This delicious improvisation was on our menu on opening day!

2 tablespoons	oil
1 cup	sliced Spanish onion
½ cup	sliced and seeded green bell pepper
½ cup	sliced and seeded red bell pepper
½ pound	firm tofu, cubed
2 medium	baked potatoes, unpeeled, cut into large pieces
1 or 2 teaspoons	tamari
	salt and pepper to taste

In a large skillet, heat the oil and sauté the onion and peppers until the onion is translucent. Add the tofu and continue cooking until the tofu is browned. Add the potatoes and cook 5 minutes more. Drizzle with tamari and add salt and pepper to taste. Serve with toast and jelly.

THE CHICAGO DINER COOKBOOK

Dairy-Free Quiche

6-8 SERVINGS

Real men do eat quiche, especially when it's heart-healthy dairy-free quiche.

1½ pounds	soft tofu, well drained
1½ pounds	firm tofu, well drained
1 cup	arrowroot or cornstarch
2 cups	water
3 tablespoons	nutritional yeast
1 tablespoon	salt
½ teaspoon	pepper
1 teaspoon	ground ginger
1 teaspoon	onion powder
½ teaspoon	nutmeg
½ teaspoon	dry mustard
3 tablespoons	sesame oil

Preheat the oven to 350°F.

Place all the ingredients into a blender or food processor, and blend until smooth. Adjust the spices to taste. Pour the mixture into an 8-inch springform pan or 9-inch pie pan, and bake 40 to 45 minutes until it springs back when lightly touched.

Variations: Add any of the following to the mixture:
- ☛ Sauteed chopped spinach, red bell pepper, and onions
- ☛ Bell peppers, onions, Mexican spices, and cilantro
- ☛ Bean sprouts, green onions, and sesame oil
- ☛ Onion and dill

Sausage Patties

ABOUT 6 SERVINGS

Spice up your scrambled eggs or tofu with this healthy sausage alternative.

1 pound	seitan		1 teaspoon	tamari
1 teaspoon	minced garlic		1 teaspoon	onion powder
¼ teaspoon	thyme		pinch	pepper
pinch	dried red pepper flakes		½ teaspoon	salt
¼ teaspoon	fennel seeds		¼ teaspoon	sage
⅓ cup	soybean oil		1 tablespoon	cornstarch
1 teaspoon	agar			

Preheat the oven to 350°F.

Grind the seitan in a food processor. In a medium bowl, mix the remaining ingredients with the ground seitan. Let rest 15 minutes, then form into patties. Pan-fry the patties in a skillet with a little oil until brown, then bake 15 to 20 minutes on a baking sheet.

Ex-Benedict

4 SERVINGS   *We call it "X-Benny." It's one of the Diner's favorites—a great specialty dish for a brunch. Serve this with Homestyle Potatoes (recipe below) and a fruit garnish.*

4   tempeh patties, cut in half horizontally
4   eggs or baked tofu slices
4   English muffins, cut in half crosswise
8   tomato slices

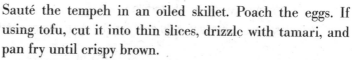

Sauté the tempeh in an oiled skillet. Poach the eggs. If using tofu, cut it into thin slices, drizzle with tamari, and pan fry until crispy brown.

Toast the muffins and top each with a tempeh slice, a poached egg or tofu slice, and 2 tomato slices. Top with Cheese Sauce (p. 134) or White Miso Sauce (p. 128).

Variations and additions:

☞   For Eggs Florentine, sauté spinach and place on top of the muffin with the other ingredients.

☞   For Homestyle Potatoes, fry cubed, unpeeled, baked potatoes in oil until browned. Season with salt and pepper.

Brunch Burrito

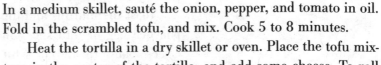

1-2 SERVINGS

There are many different ways to make burritos. Any vegetable of choice can be sautéed for a filling, or try stuffing it with ground seitan, potatoes, onions, peppers, and cheese. Be creative!!

2 tablespoons	chopped onion
2 tablespoons	chopped green or red bell pepper
2 tablespoons	chopped tomato
1 tablespoon	oil
1 cup	Scrambled Tofu (p. 94)
1 large	whole wheat tortilla
1 tablespoon	shredded mild cheddar cheese (dairy or nondairy)

In a medium skillet, sauté the onion, pepper, and tomato in oil. Fold in the scrambled tofu, and mix. Cook 5 to 8 minutes.

Heat the tortilla in a dry skillet or oven. Place the tofu mixture in the center of the tortilla, and add some cheese. To roll up, fold the bottom part of the tortilla over the mix, and roll the sides over to tightly close. Brown the burrito seam side down in a lightly oiled skillet. Serve with spicy puréed beans, rice, and salsa.

Banana Poppyseed Bread

MAKES 1 LOAF

Quick breads are inexpensive. Try using a narrow 4 x 10-inch pan available at specialty stores to make tea-style slices. This can also be baked in muffin tins.

1 cup	unbleached flour
1 cup	whole wheat pastry flour
1½ teaspoons	baking powder
½ teaspoon	baking soda
¼ cup	poppy seeds
½ cup	walnuts (optional)
½ cup	turbinado sugar or other sweetener
2	ripe bananas, mashed
⅓ cup	oil
½ cup	soymilk with 1 teaspoon lemon juice added
1 teaspoon	vanilla extract

Preheat the oven to 350°F.

Mix the dry ingredients in a large bowl. In a separate bowl, mash the bananas, and stir in all the remaining liquids. Add the wet ingredients to the dry ingredients, and mix together. Pour into an oiled 4 x 8-inch bread pan, and bake 50 minutes.

Diner Cornbread Muffins

10-12 MUFFINS

At the Chicago Diner, we serve our corn muffins with every entrée—they are that popular! Serve warm with a little soy margarine and honey. Nothing better! Great for breakfast as well.

1 cup	cornmeal
½ cup	pastry flour
½ cup	unbleached flour
2½ teaspoons	baking powder
1 teaspoon	baking soda
1 cup	water (for a richer flavor, substitute soymilk for half the water)
2 tablespoons	oil
1 tablespoon	turbinado sugar

Preheat the oven to 375°F. Stir the dry ingredients, except the sugar, in a medium mixing bowl. In another bowl, combine the water, oil, and sugar, and stir well. Add the wet ingredients to the dry ingredients, and mix. Pour the batter into oiled cupcake tins ⅔ full. Bake 20 to 25 minutes.

Focaccia

1 COOKIE SHEET *A famous Italian flat bread with many variations.*

2 cups	warm water (110°F)
2½ teaspoons	yeast
2 teaspoons	barley malt, raw sugar, or honey
3 tablespoons	olive oil
1½ teaspoons	salt
1 to 2 tablespoons	dried rosemary
1 cup	whole wheat flour
5 cups	unbleached flour

In a medium bowl, mix together the warm water, yeast, and sweetener. Stir and let stand 5 minutes, until the yeast is bubbly. Stir in the oil, salt, rosemary, and flours. In a mixer fitted with a dough hook, knead 5 to 10 minutes. Let rise 45 minutes to 1 hour in a covered bowl, punch down, and let rise again.

Preheat the oven to 400°F. Roll out the dough onto a sheet pan, and drizzle with olive oil. Prick the bread with a fork. Bake 25 to 30 minutes.

If you like, sprinkle with black olives, onions, or tomato puree.

Irish Soda Bread

1 LOAF   *A fast, easy, and light quick bread, speckled with currants and caraway seeds.*

1 cup	whole wheat flour
2 cups	unbleached flour
1 teaspoon	baking powder
1½ teaspoons	baking soda
pinch	salt
2 tablespoons	turbinado sugar
⅓ cup	currants (optional)
1 tablespoon	caraway seeds (optional)
2 cups	soymilk
3 tablespoons	lemon juice or vinegar

Preheat the oven to 350°F.

Combine the dry ingredients in a medium mixing bowl, including the currants and caraway seeds, if using. Mix well and add soymilk and lemon juice. Mix until a wet dough forms. Place the dough onto a floured board or countertop, and knead 2 to 3 minutes, just until the dough sticks together. Form into a round loaf and slice an "X" into the top of the dough with a sharp knife. (Myth has it this "lets the fairies out" while baking.) Bake on an oiled cookie sheet 20 to 25 minutes.

Basic Wheat Bread

3 LOAVES *A two-step approach. This bread is fine and light, perfect for sandwiches.*

SPONGE :

4 cups	warm water
2 tablespoons	sweetener (your choice)
2 tablespoons	dry yeast
2 cups	whole wheat flour

Mix the ingredients together well in a large bowl. At this time, you may add your choice of cinnamon, raisins, more sweetener, sesame seeds, and/or oatmeal. Let sit in a warm place 20 to 30 minutes. Add to sponge bowl:

DOUGH :

½ cup	oil
2 teaspoons	salt
4 to 5 cups	flour (add gradually)

Knead 5 to 10 minutes.

Transfer the dough to a lightly floured work surface, and knead until springy and no longer sticky. Place the dough in a large, oiled bowl, cover with a clean towel, and let rise in a warm place for 1 hour. Punch down and let rise again.

Preheat oven to 350°F. On a work surface, knead the dough into a ball and divide into thirds. Place in oiled loaf pans or form into rounds on baking sheets, and bake 50 minutes to 1 hour, or until the bread sounds hollow when turned out of the pan and thumped on the bottom with your finger.

Fruit Preserves

ABOUT 3 CUPS *A healthful alternative to store-bought jellies and jams, and not to mention a lot tastier! This is also a good filling or frosting for cookies and cakes.*

1½ cups	dried apricots, prunes or mixed fruit
1 or 2 tablespoons	honey

Soak the fruit overnight in warm water. Drain. Purée in a food processor with the honey.

Fruit Salsa

4 CUPS *Serve with crisp cinnamon tortilla chips (see below).*

½ medium	cantaloupe, chopped
½ medium	honeydew melon, chopped
1 cup	orange juice
	orange zest
¼ bunch	cilantro, chopped

Toss all the ingredients together and chill.

Variation: Add sliced strawberries, or toss in some pomegranate seeds for a winter holiday treat.

☛   For Cinnamon Tortillas: Preheat the oven to 300°F. Cut whole wheat tortillas into triangle shapes, brush with oil, and sprinkle with cinnamon and sugar. Bake on a sheet pan for 10 to 15 minutes.

THE VEGETARIAN
Soups
CHICAGO DINER

Basic Vegetable Broth

Miso Soup

Garden Vegetable Miso Soup

Minestrone

French Onion Soup

Pasta Fagioli

Lentil Soup

Gazpacho

Black Bean Soup

Cream of Potato-Leek Soup

Carrot-Dill Soup

Squash Apple Soup

Adzuki/Shiitake Soup

Cream of Broccoli Soup

Split Pea Soup

Corn Chowder

Bean Grain Medley Soup

Basic Vegetable Broth

ABOUT 3-4 QUARTS

The more vegetables you use, the richer the stock will be, but avoid the cabbage family.

1	onion, peeled
1	carrot, peeled
1	stalk celery, with leaves
2	sprigs parsley
1	teaspoon salt
4 or 5	peppercorns
¼ cup	nutritional yeast
1	bay leaf
2	whole cloves

Place all the ingredients in a large pot with enough water to cover 1½ times (2 to 3 quarts). Cover and simmer about 1 hour. Strain.

Miso Soup

4-6 SERVINGS

This basic soup is ready to serve immediately. You don't want to boil this soup, for miso is a live food, and boiling kills the enzymes.

6 cups	hot water
⅓ cup	white or yellow miso
½ cup	tofu cubes
1 tablespoon	diced scallions
	shredded nori for garnish (optional)

In a medium pot, bring the water to a boil. Remove the pot from the heat, and add the remaining ingredients. Garnish with shredded nori before serving.

Garden Vegetable Miso Soup

4-6 SERVINGS   *This is known as the pick-me-up soup!*

1½ quarts	water
1 small	onion, diced
2 cups	thinly sliced cabbage
1	carrot, julienned
1 or 2	stalks celery, sliced diagonally
¼ cup	ginger juice*
3 tablespoons	miso
2 teaspoons	sesame oil (optional)
	chopped parsley for garnish

Bring the water to a boil in a large pot. Add the vegetables to the boiling water, and simmer 5 to 8 minutes. Turn off the heat and add the ginger juice. Remove 2 cups of broth from the soup pot. Stir the miso into the broth until it dissolves, then add back to the soup. Adjust the flavors and add the parsley before serving.

Variation: Sauté the vegetables in the sesame oil, then add to the boiling water.

*To make ginger juice, place 2 to 3 small ginger root slices in a blender with enough water to cover. Blend 1 to 2 minutes, and strain juice.

Minestrone

An old favorite standby, this recipe makes lots.

½ cup	dried navy beans	2 stalks	celery, diced
½ cup	dried red beans	1 (15-ounce) can	tomatoes
½ cup	dried lima beans	2 tablespoons	minced garlic
6 quarts	water or vegetable stock	2 tablespoons	oregano
2	bay leaves	2 tablespoons	basil
2 medium	potatoes, diced	1 tablespoon	salt
2	carrots, diced	1 small	bell pepper, diced
1 large	onion, diced	1 cup	cooked pasta
1½ cups	thinly sliced cabbage	2 cups	chopped fresh spinach
1 small	zucchini, diced		

In a very large pot, bring the beans to a boil in the water with the bay leaves. Reduce the heat and simmer about 1 hour. When the beans are almost tender, add the potatoes, carrots, and onion. Cook until tender. Add cabbage, zucchini, celery, tomatoes, and seasonings. Cover and simmer 30 minutes more. Season to taste with salt and pepper.

Add some cooked pasta and chopped spinach upon serving. Serve with a salad, crispy bread, and a nice glass of red wine on a chilly winter night.

French Onion Soup

4-6 SERVINGS *This classic is so great and so inexpensive!*

2 to 3 tablespoons	oil
3 large	Spanish onions, cut in half-moon slices
1 teaspoon	thyme
1	bay leaf
1 teaspoon	oregano
1 teaspoon	basil
1½ quarts	hot Vegetable Broth (p 40) or hot water
3 tablespoons	flour (or as needed) to thicken soup
3 tablespoons	dark miso
¼ cup	tamari (optional)
2 teaspoons	salt
¼ teaspoon	pepper

Heat the oil in a large pot, and add the onions and herbs. Cook until the onions are caramelized, about 15 minutes. Add a little flour while stirring to avoid lumps. Then add the hot broth or water. Simmer 15 minutes. Remove 2 cups of broth from the soup pot. Stir the miso into the broth until it dissolves, then add back to the soup. Add tamari, salt, and pepper.

Gazpacho

6-8 SERVINGS

Our version is a chunky, crispy soup, great as an appetizer or on hot summer days. Serve with crispy bread and a nice glass of white wine.

1 medium	onion, finely diced
2 medium	cucumbers, peeled, seeded, and chopped
1 to 2 stalks	celery, diced
2 medium	bell peppers, diced
5 large	tomatoes, diced
2 medium cloves	garlic, minced
2 teaspoons	salt
1 teaspoon	oregano
1 teaspoon	cumin
¼ teaspoon	pepper
2 cups	tomato juice, plus more as needed
1 cup	water
2 tablespoons	olive oil
2 tablespoons	lemon juice
¼ cup	red wine vinegar

In a large bowl, combine all of the ingredients. Adjust the flavors to taste. If the soup is too thick, add more tomato juice. Cover and chill at least 1 hour before serving.

Black Bean Soup

4-6 SERVINGS   *Hearty and heart-warming—comfort food at its best.*

2 cups	dried black beans
8 cups	water
1	bay leaf
1 piece	kombu
1 medium	onion, diced
1 medium	bell pepper, diced
2 teaspoons	cumin
1 teaspoon	oregano
1 teaspoon	coriander
1 teaspoon	chili powder
3 cloves	garlic, minced
1 tablespoon	red wine vinegar
1 tablespoon	honey or sugar
	Dairy-Free Sour Cream (p. 126), chopped green onions, and chopped cilantro for garnish

In a large pot, soak the beans overnight. Discard the soaking water. Rinse the beans and return them to the pot. Add 8 cups cold water, the bay leaf, and kombu. Bring to a boil, reduce the heat and simmer, partially covered, for 1 hour. When the beans are almost tender, add the vegetables and herbs. Simmer until the vegetables are cooked, about 30 minutes more. Stir in the vinegar and honey. Purée the soup until smooth directly in the pot with an immersion blender, or blend small amounts in a blender. Garnish.

Cream of Potato-Leek Soup

6-8 SERVINGS   *A delicate, creamy soup; fast, easy, and delicious hot or chilled.*

2	leeks
2½ quarts	water
2 large	Vidalia onions, diced
6 to 8 large	red potatoes, diced
1 tablespoon	minced garlic
	salt to taste
	white pepper to taste
1 tablespoon	chopped dill

Remove most of the green on the leeks; discard. Slice leeks lengthwise and slice thin crosswise. Rinse thoroughly to remove soil.

Bring the water to a boil, add the onions and potatoes, and cook until tender. Add the leeks and garlic, and simmer 10 minutes more. Add the salt, pepper, and dill. Cook, stirring occasionally, until smooth.

For a richer flavor, you can add a little nutritional yeast and soymilk.

Variations: Substitute 6 cups broccoli or cauliflower for the leeks. Do not overcook the broccoli, or it will turn the soup a brownish color.

Carrot-Dill Soup

ABOUT 6 SERVINGS

Even Bugs Bunny has his ears up for this delight. Good served hot or cold.

1 tablespoon	canola or vegetable oil
6 to 7	carrots, chopped
1 large	onion, chopped
2 cloves	garlic, chopped
1 teaspoon	salt
¼ teaspoon	pepper
2 cups	vegetable stock or canned broth
	dill, nutmeg, curry, or ginger (optional)
2 cups	soymilk, dairy milk, or cream

In a large saucepan, heat the oil over medium heat. Add the carrots and onion, and cook approximately 5 minutes. Add the garlic, salt, pepper, and stock, along with the optional seasonings, if using, and bring to a boil. Reduce the heat to medium-low, cover, and simmer about 20 minutes.

Transfer the mixture to a blender or food processor, and purée. Return the purée to the pan, and add the soymilk. Heat the mixture carefully. (The soymilk will curdle if boiled.)

Squash Apple Soup

6 SERVINGS *A creamy-style soup with a nice autumn flair.*

2 tablespoons	vegetable oil
4 cups	cooked squash (acorn, butternut, carnival, or delicata)
1 small	onion, diced
1	Granny Smith apple, peeled and diced
1 stalk	celery, diced
	seasonings of your choice (see below)
¼ cup	mirin
4 cups	apple cider or apple juice
2 tablespoons	arrowroot to thicken (if needed)
	salt and pepper to taste
4 to 6 cups	vegetable broth

Heat the oil in a large saucepan. Add the remaining ingredients and bring to a boil. Reduce the heat to medium-low, and simmer, covered, about 20 minutes.

This soup can be served in many different variations. Here are a few:

☛ Transfer all the ingredients into a blender, and purée. Float some sliced apples on top as a garnish.

☛ Leave the vegetables chunky, and serve thick.

☛ Purée half the soup and add the chunky vegetables to the puréed mixture.

☛ Seasonings to add to the broth: rosemary, nutmeg, sage, clove, thyme, cinnamon, bay leaf, ginger

☛ Substitute baked squash for raw squash, or use 1 (15-ounce) can pumpkin purée.

Adzuki-Shiitake Soup

6 SERVINGS

Add a little grated fresh ginger to each serving for a delightful spicy touch.

1 cup	dry adzuki beans, sorted, rinsed, and soaked overnight
7 to 8 cups	water
1	carrot, diced
1 medium	onion, sliced
1 cup	chopped bok choy, diagonally cut
1 to 2 cloves	garlic, minced
1 tablespoon	sesame oil
1 cup	sliced fresh shiitake mushrooms, stemmed
2 to 3 tablespoons	white or yellow miso
1 to 2 tablespoons	tamari
pinch	cayenne pepper

In a large pot, bring the beans and water to a boil. Cover and simmer 1 to 1½ hours or until almost tender. Sauté the carrot and onion with the bok choy and garlic in oil until tender. Add the shiitake and cook until everything is almost tender. Add to the bean pot, adding more water or stock if necessary. Remove 1 cup broth from the soup pot. Stir the miso into the broth until it dissolves, then add back to the soup. Add tamari and cayenne, and adjust seasonings to taste.

Cream of Broccoli Soup

6-8 SERVINGS

So fresh, so creamy, dreamy smooth, excellent served chilled. You can also substitute cauliflower or asparagus for the broccoli. The asparagus makes a spring green soup—it shouts out in your bowl!

2 pounds	chopped broccoli
1 medium	onion, chopped
1 clove	garlic, minced
4 cups	vegetable broth or water
2½ cups	soymilk
1 teaspoon	salt
¼ teaspoon	white pepper
¼ cup	unbleached flour
¼ cup	nutritional yeast (optional)

Place all the ingredients except the flour and 1 cup of the broccoli into a large pot, and bring to a boil. Simmer 15 minutes.

Place the mixture in a food processor with the flour, and blend until smooth. Pour the mixture back into the pot with the reserved broccoli, and simmer until it thickens. Adjust the seasonings to taste.

Split Pea Soup

8 SERVINGS *Try topping off this thick and hearty soup with crunchy croutons.*

2 cups	yellow or green split peas
2	bay leaves
3 quarts	water
1 medium	potato, diced
1½ cups	chopped onion
¾ cup	finely diced carrots
¾ cup	chopped celery
1 tablespoon	salt
½ teaspoon	pepper
¼ teaspoon	marjoram
¼ teaspoon	caraway seeds
	croutons for garnish

Combine the peas and bay leaves with the water in a large soup pot, and bring to a boil. Cover and simmer about 3 minutes. Turn off the heat and let sit 30 minutes to 1 hour. Add the potato, onion, and carrots, and cook until tender. Add the remaining ingredients and cook 30 minutes more. Add water or broth as needed. Garnish with croutons.

Corn Chowder

If you want to make any soup really thick, you can add arrowroot. Always mix the arrowroot with cold water and make a slurry before adding to the soup. Start with 2 to 3 tablespoons arrowroot mixed with 5 to 6 tablespoons water.

2 tablespoons	vegetable oil
1 large	onion, diced
1	bay leaf
1 pound	potatoes, peeled and diced
2 to 3 sprigs	thyme
	salt to taste
1 quart	vegetable stock or water
1 large	red bell pepper, diced
4 cups	corn kernels
2 to 3 cups	soymilk
	salt, pepper, and nutmeg to taste

In a large soup pot, heat the oil and sauté the onion and bay leaf until soft, about 10 minutes. Add the potatoes, thyme, salt, and stock, and simmer until the potatoes are tender, about 20 minutes. Add the bell pepper, corn, and soymilk, and simmer until heated through. If the soup needs a little more thickness, stir in some arrowroot or cornstarch. Season to taste with salt, pepper, and nutmeg.

Bean-Grain Medley Soup

8-10 SERVINGS

Thick and rich; accompany with some good bread and a salad for a satisfying supper.

6 to 8 cups	water or stock
2 or 3	bay leaves
1½ cups	dried lentils
¾ cup	dried split peas
¾ cup	barley
¾ cup	rice
⅓ cup	dried navy beans
½ pound	onions, diced
½ pound	mushrooms, sliced
¼ pound	celery, chopped
2 cloves	garlic
1 tablespoon	chili powder
	salt and pepper to taste
¼ cup	tamari

In a stock pot, heat the water or stock with the bay leaves. Add the beans and grains, and bring to a boil. Cover and simmer 45 minutes. Add the remaining ingredients, cover, and simmer 30 minutes more. Season to taste.

56

Salads & Dressings
THE VEGETARIAN CHICAGO DINER

Land and Sea

French Lentil Salad

Portobello-Tofu Salad

Santa Fe Black Bean Salad

Cilantro-Lime Vinaigrette

Tempeh Salad

Jicama Salad

Japanese Noodle Salad

Perfect Potato Salad

Oriental Rice Salad

Tabbouleh

Quinoa-Orange Salad

Sun Salad

Marinated Italian
Vegetables

Curry Cashew Pasta Salad

Lemon-Parsley Dressing

Orange Flair Dressing

Creamy Garlic Dressing

Cucumber Dressing

Caesar Dressing

Quick Reuben Sauce

Honey-Poppyseed Dressing

Quick Salsa

Oriental Vinaigrette

Tahini Dressing

Rosy Beet Dressing

Pesto

Italian Herb Dressing

4 SERVINGS — *A coleslaw variation in a fresh, gingery dressing. You can use any other vegetable of your choice, such as napa cabbage, beets, celery, etc.*

1	carrot, grated
2 cups	shredded green cabbage
1 cup	shredded red cabbage
¼ cup	diced green onion
⅓ cup	chopped parsley
1 cup	arame, soaked, rinsed, and drained

Combine all the ingredients in a medium bowl, and toss with Oriental Vinaigrette (p. 77). Garnish with gomasio (p. 72).

French Lentil Salad

A light refreshing meal; serve over spinach greens.

SALAD:		**VINAIGRETTE:**	
1 large	red pepper	½ cup	olive oil
	oil	¼ cup	lemon juice
5 to 6 cups	water	2 cloves	garlic, minced
1 cup	dried French lentils	½ teaspoon	salt
1	bay leaf	⅛ teaspoon	pepper
1 medium	onion, diced	pinch	cayenne
1 small	carrot, diced	¼ teaspoon	paprika
2 stalks	celery, diced	½ teaspoon	marjoram
		1 teaspoon	fresh thyme

Preheat the oven to 350°F. Brush the pepper with oil, place on a baking sheet, and bake for 20 to 25 minutes. Remove the pepper from the oven, and place it in a bowl. Cover with plastic and set aside. When cool, peel the skin, remove the seeds, and slice.

In a medium pot, bring the water, lentils, and bay leaf to a boil. Cook until the lentils are tender. Drain and place in serving bowl. Add the sliced red peppers and remaining vegetables. Whisk the vinaigrette ingredients together, and stir into the salad. Best when served at room temperature.

Portobello-Tofu Salad

8-10 SERVINGS *The best of the best—tasty all year long.*

12 ounces	firm tofu, cut in large cubes
2 tablespoons	tamari
2 tablespoons	olive oil
6	portobello mushroom caps
1 large	red bell pepper, halved and seeded
1 large	onion, sliced into 4 or 5 circles
	Pesto (p. 79) or olive oil, salt, and pepper
¼ cup	balsamic vinegar
	pepper to taste
¼ bunch	fresh parsley, chopped

Preheat the oven to 350°F. Toss the tofu cubes with tamari and oil, and pour out onto a baking sheet. Bake approximately 25 minutes.

Brush mushrooms, bell pepper, and onion with your favorite pesto or olive oil plus salt and pepper. Panfry 8 to 10 minutes or bake 15 to 20 minutes. When cool, slice mushrooms and bell peppers lengthwise, and toss with baked tofu cubes, balsamic vinegar, pepper, and parsley.

Best when served at room temperature, not chilled.

Really yummy. Use pesto on pg. 79.

Santa Fe Black Bean Salad

4 SERVINGS   *A lunchtime, summertime favorite. Olé!*

5 cups	water	1½ teaspoons	cumin
1¼ cups	dried black beans	½ cup	diced red bell peppers
1	bay leaf	¼ cup	sliced green onions
1 clove	garlic, minced		Cilantro Lime Vinaigrette (below)
½ teaspoon	salt		mixed greens
		1	avocado, sliced, for garnish

In a large pot, bring the water, beans, and bay leaf to a boil. Cover and simmer 1½ hours. Drain; place in a medium bowl. Add the garlic, salt, cumin, peppers, and green onions. Toss with Cilantro-Lime Vinaigrette, and serve over mixed greens, garnished with avocado slices.

Cilantro–Lime Vinaigrette

ABOUT 3/4 CUP   *This dressing goes great on chilled pasta salads, too!*

4 tablespoons	lime juice
6 tablespoons	olive oil
1 tablespoon	turbinado sugar
½ teaspoon	salt
¼ teaspoon	pepper
2 tablespoons	chopped cilantro

Place all the ingredients in a small bowl and whisk.

Tempeh Salad

4-6 SERVINGS

This salad is number one with our manager Lara. It is so versatile! You can stuff it into pita bread or a ripe tomato, wrap it up in your favorite tortilla, or simply eat it as is.

2 tablespoons	oil
1 pound	tempeh, diced small
1 tablespoon	tamari
¼ cup	diced green onions
2 tablespoons	chopped parsley
¼ cup	grated carrot (optional)
1 tablespoon	chopped fresh basil
1½ cups	eggless mayonnaise

Heat the oil in a medium skillet over medium heat, and sauté the chopped tempeh 5 to 10 minutes. When golden brown, remove from the heat and stir in the soy sauce. Cool. In a medium mixing bowl, add all the ingredients and mix well. Cover and chill.

Jicama Salad

4 SERVINGS

Often referred to as the Mexican potato, this crunchy, sweet root vegetable is filled with vitamin C and potassium. It is most readily available in the United States from November through May.

1 medium	jicama, peeled and julienned or cut into strips
2	oranges, peeled and sectioned
1	avocado, diced
1 small	red onion, peeled and sliced into half circles
1 medium	seedless cucumber, cut in half lengthwise and sliced crosswise
2 tablespoons	chopped cilantro, parsley, or mint
½ cup	orange juice
¼ cup	lemon juice
¼ cup	olive oil
	salt and pepper to taste

Combine all the ingredients and mix well. Serve as is or on a bed of greens.

Japanese Noodle Salad

6-10 SERVINGS   *A nice party fun food and Asian delight.*

2 cups	sugar snap peas, strings removed, and julienned
1 cup	sliced shiitake mushrooms
1 large	red bell pepper, julienned
2 cups	cauliflower florets
⅓ cup	arame, soaked, rinsed, drained, and patted dry
½ bunch	green onions, diagonally cut
2 cups	bean sprouts (optional)

VINAIGRETTE:	
1 tablespoon	soy sauce
¼ cup	mirin
2 teaspoons	ginger juice* or grated ginger
⅓ cup	rice vinegar
⅓ cup	lightly toasted sesame oil
1 teaspoon	salt
⅛ teaspoon	cayenne pepper

1 (12-ounce) package	udon or soba noodles, cooked
1 teaspoon	sesame oil

Place the vegetables, except green onions and sprouts, briefly in a large pot of boiling water and then under cold water to stop the cooking process; drain. Combine with the green onions, sprouts, and noodles, and toss with the sesame oil.

Mix all the vinaigrette ingredients together in a large bowl. Toss with noodle mixture. Refrigerate until ready to serve.

*To make ginger juice, place 2 to 3 small ginger root slices in a blender with enough water to cover. Blend 1 to 2 minutes, and strain juice.

Perfect Potato Salad

6 servings

Why so perfect? Because this potato salad, unlike its traditional counterpart, is cholesterol-free! Be sure to cook the potatoes in separate pots; sweet potatoes cook more quickly than white potatoes.

6 medium	potatoes, boiled, peeled (if using baby reds, don't peel), and cubed
2 to 3 medium	sweet potatoes, boiled, peeled, and cubed
½ cup	diced onion
⅓ cup	diced celery
½ cup	diced red bell pepper
¼ cup	chopped parsley
	salt and pepper to taste
¾ to 1 cup	eggless mayonnaise

Combine all the ingredients in a medium bowl. Mix together and season to taste. Serve well chilled

Oriental Rice Salad

6 SERVINGS   *A delicate light-tasting salad that is so colorful! Don't forget your chopsticks.*

4 cups	cold cooked brown rice
¼ cup	sesame oil
2 tablespoons	mirin
⅓ cup	rice vinegar
1 teaspoon	salt
½ teaspoon	pepper
1 medium	carrot, julienned
3	green onions, chopped
½ cup	snow peas, julienned
½ cup	diced red bell pepper
1 cup	bean sprouts, drained
1 stalk	celery, diagonally cut
2 tablespoons	chopped parsley
½ cup	corn kernels (optional)

Place the rice in a large mixing bowl. In a small bowl, combine the oil, mirin, rice vinegar, salt, and pepper. Stir and pour over the rice. Add the remaining ingredients and toss well.

Tabbouleh

3-4 SERVINGS *Summer picnics are a great place to bring this tangy salad. Serve it with a little Baba Ghanouj (p. 12), Hummus (p. 11), and pita bread.*

2 cups	water
1 cup	bulghur wheat
2 medium	tomatoes, diced
¼ cup	chopped green onions
2 cups	chopped fresh parsley
1 medium	cucumber, peeled, seeded, and chopped
3 tablespoons	olive oil
4 tablespoons	lemon juice
1 teaspoon	salt
pinch	pepper
1 tablespoon	chopped fresh mint, or 1 teaspoon dried mint

In a medium pot, bring the water to a boil, and add the bulghur. Remove from the heat, cover, and let stand 15 minutes. Drain. Put the bulghur into a medium bowl, and add the rest of the ingredients. Stir and chill.

Quinoa-Orange Salad

4-6 SERVINGS *Chock-full of the Mother Earth grain, most nutritious with our tangy Orange Flair Dressing (p. 73)*

1½ cups	quinoa
3 cups	water
½ cup	chopped dried mixed fruit
⅓ cup	coarsely chopped almonds
2 stalks	celery, diagonally cut
2 tablespoons	chopped parsley
2 to 3	orange segments
½ to ⅔ cup	Orange Flair Dressing (p. 73)

Rinse the quinoa in a fine strainer. In a medium pot, bring the water to a boil and add the quinoa. Stir, cover, and simmer on low heat 25 minutes; drain any remaining water.

In a smaller pan, place the dried fruit in boiling water (enough to cover the fruit), and boil 5 to 10 minutes. Drain. Toast the almonds in a dry skillet or oven until they give off a toasted nutty smell. In a medium bowl, combine all ingredients and toss well.

Sun Salad

The only thing better than the way our eggless egg salad tastes is the fact that it is cholesterol-free. This salad can be used any way you use egg salad. Stuff it into a pita, make a sandwich or wrap, or serve over greens or with crackers.

1½ pounds	firm tofu, drained and diced small
½ to 1 cup	eggless mayonnaise
¼ cup	diced onion
1 to 2	stalks celery, diced
½ cup	chopped parsley
⅓ cup	diced red or green bell peppers
⅓ cup	toasted sunflower seeds (see below)
½ teaspoon	salt
¼ teaspoon	pepper
½ teaspoon	dry mustard
¼ teaspoon	turmeric
2 tablespoons	pickle relish (optional)

Combine all the ingredients and refrigerate. Best served well chilled.

Note: To toast sunflower seeds, cook in a dry skillet over medium heat until aromatic. Remove from the pan immediately.

Marinated Italian Vegetables

6-8 SERVINGS   *This makes a wonderful summertime side dish.*

DRESSING:

½ cup	olive oil
½ cup	soybean oil
½ cup	wine vinegar
2 teaspoons	oregano
1 teaspoon	salt
½ teaspoon	pepper
1 teaspoon	basil

SALAD:

1 pint	cherry tomatoes, halved
2	green bell peppers, diced large
1	red bell pepper, diced large
1 medium	red onion, sliced
½ pound	mushrooms, quartered or halved
1 cup	black olives, halved
1 cup	cooked garbanzo beans
1 cup	cooked kidney beans

Whisk the ingredients for the dressing, and set aside. Combine the vegetables and beans. Toss with the dressing and refrigerate for at least 1 hour before serving.

Curry Cashew Pasta Salad

6-8 SERVINGS *A yellow glow of a salad with its honey sesame dressing.*

VINAIGRETTE:

¾ cup	apple cider vinegar
½ cup	soybean oil
¼ cup	sesame oil
¼ cup	honey
¼ cup	ginger juice*
1 teaspoon	cumin powder
2 teaspoons	curry powder
1 teaspoon	garlic powder
½ teaspoon	turmeric
1 teaspoon	salt
pinch	cayenne

SALAD

2 to 3	carrots, julienned
½ head	cauliflower, in florets
2 to 3	green onions, chopped
1 medium	red bell pepper, chopped
1 medium	green bell pepper, chopped
1 cup	black olives, sliced
⅓ cup	raisins
⅓ cup	toasted cashew halves
12 ounces	rotini, cooked, drained, and set aside

Mix all the vinaigrette ingredients in a blender, and set aside.

Place carrots and cauliflower briefly in boiling salted water, then under cold water to stop the cooking process; drain. Mix with all remaining salad ingredients, except the pasta, in a large bowl. Add pasta and vinaigrette, and toss well. Chill.

*To make ginger juice, place 2 to 3 small ginger root slices in a blender with enough water to cover. Blend 1 to 2 minutes, and strain juice.

Lemon-Parsley Dressing

ABOUT 2 1/2 CUPS

This dressing is number one with our guests at the restaurant because it's so light, allowing the flavors of your salad to come through. The sesame seed, salt, and kelp powder mix is a traditional Japanese condiment called gomasio (see p. 155).

GOMASIO:

1 cup	raw sesame seeds
2 teaspoons	salt
1 teaspoon	kelp powder (optional)

DRESSING:

½ cup	gomasio
⅔ cup	water
⅔ cup	lemon juice
⅔ cup	olive oil
2 tablespoons	chopped fresh parsley
1 to 2 tablespoons	tamari

To make the gomasio, heat the sesame seeds, salt and kelp powder in a dry skillet on medium-high heat 3 to 5 minutes. Stir often, for it will burn easily. When the seeds pop and get brown, they are done. Remove from the heat and cool.

Place the gomasio in a blender or food processor, and grind 2 to 3 minutes. Remove all but ½ cup of the gomasio from the blender, add all the remaining ingredients to the blender, and process thoroughly. Store the extra gomasio in a glass container for use in other recipes, such as Land and Sea Salad (p. 58) or to spice up basic brown rice (p. 92).

Orange Flair Dressing

2 CUPS *The citrus flavor makes a green salad tangy and zesty.*

¾ cup | orange juice
1 teaspoon | orange zest
1 cup | olive oil
2 tablespoons | lemon juice
| salt and pepper to taste

Place all the ingredients in a blender, and mix well. Season to taste and refrigerate. Best when served well chilled.

Creamy Garlic Dressing

1 3/4 CUPS *To create this creamy dressing, make certain that you do not blend the mayonnaise, for it will turn into liquid.*

1 cup | soymilk
2 teaspoons | lemon juice
3 to 4 cloves | garlic, minced
⅔ cup | eggless mayonnaise
2 tablespoons | chopped parsley
pinch | salt

Place the soymilk, lemon juice, and garlic in a blender, and process until the mixture is smooth like milk and the garlic is not chunky. Pour into a bowl and add the rest of the ingredients. Stir well and season to taste.

Cucumber Dressing

ABOUT 3 CUPS   *Great as a dip, salad dressing, or on sandwiches.*

1 medium	seedless cucumber
12 ounces	soft tofu, drained well
¼ cup	chopped green onions
½ cup	chopped parsley
½ cup	soymilk
¼ cup	lemon juice
1½ teaspoons	salt
¼ teaspoon	pepper
1 teaspoon	dried dill weed

Cut the cucumber into large chunks.
Combine the cucumber chunks with the
rest of the ingredients in a blender,
and blend until creamy.

Caesar Dressing

3 CUPS *Dairy-free, anchovy-free, delicious!*

⅓ cup	arame
1 cup	extra-virgin olive oil
¼ cup	soft tofu
½ cup	lemon juice
½ cup	water
1 teaspoon	minced garlic
½ teaspoon	salt
½ teaspoon	pepper

Soak, rinse, and drain the arame. Place in a blender with the rest of the ingredients, and mix for about 3 minutes.

Quick Reuben Sauce

2 1/2 CUPS *This recipe makes a great sauce for sandwiches or Thousand Island dressing for salads.*

½ cup	finely chopped pickles
1 cup	eggless mayonnaise
⅔ cup	catsup

Mix all the ingredients together in a bowl.

Honey-Poppyseed Dressing

2 CUPS — *A sweet dressing that's great for fruit salad dishes.*

1¼ cups	soy oil
½ cup	apple cider vinegar
1 tablespoon	chopped onion
¼ cup	honey
1 teaspoon	poppy seeds
½ teaspoon	salt
2 teaspoons	dry mustard

Place all the ingredients in a blender, and blend until creamy smooth. (The dressing will turn white.)

Quick Salsa

4 SERVINGS — *Always a favorite, quick and easy, make it mild or hot.*

1 (28-ounce) can	tomatoes (whole or crushed)
3 tablespoons	freshly squeezed lemon or lime juice
2 tablespoons	cilantro
½ teaspoon	salt
½ teaspoon	cumin
1 small	jalapeño pepper, seeded and chopped

Place all the ingredients in a blender, and process a few seconds.

Oriental Vinaigrette

ABOUT 2/3 CUP — *An aromatic dressing; use on Asian vegetables, greens, noodles, sea vegetables, grilled tofu....*

¼ cup	sesame oil
2 tablespoons	mirin
⅓ cup	rice vinegar
1 teaspoon	salt
½ teaspoon	pepper

In a small bowl, whisk all the ingredients together.

Tahini Dressing

1 1/2 CUPS — *This is a classic dipping sauce as well as a dressing. Try it tossed into blanched, chilled veggies.*

½ cup	tahini
⅓ cup	water
⅓ cup	lemon juice
2 teaspoons	minced garlic
¼ teaspoon	salt

In a small bowl, whisk all the ingredients together.

Rosy Beet Dressing

ABOUT 2 1/2 CUPS

"Pretty in pink" and good for you.

1 cup	soft tofu
¼ cup	chopped cooked beets
¼ cup	mirin
1 tablespoon	white miso
½ cup	rice wine vinegar
1 teaspoon	salt
¼ teaspoon	pepper
¼ to ½ cup	water

Place all the ingredients in a blender, and process until creamy.

Pesto

ABOUT 2 CUPS

In the summertime when the ingredients are plentiful from the garden, you can make and freeze this great spread to use later in soups, sauces, or as a bread topping.

2 cups	basil leaves
1 cup	spinach leaves
½ cup	chopped parsley leaves
1 to 2 tablespoons	crushed garlic
½ teaspoon	salt
¼ teaspoon	pepper
½ to ⅔ cup	olive oil

Put all the ingredients, except the olive oil, into a blender or food processor, and mix on low. Slowly drizzle olive oil into the blender as you process, creating a thin paste.

Variation: Add ⅓ cup pine nuts, walnuts, sunflower seeds, or Parmesan cheese.

Italian Herb Dressing

ABOUT 3/4 CUP *Great for pasta salads or potato salads.*

1 to 2 cloves	garlic, minced
1 teaspoon	marjoram
1 teaspoon	basil
1 teaspoon	oregano
1 teaspoon	salt
¼ teaspoon	pepper
1 teaspoon	dry mustard
½ cup	olive oil
2 to 3 tablespoons	red wine vinegar

Mix all the ingredients together very well in a blender, or just shake in a jar with a tight lid. Chill. Shake before serving.

Greens & Grains

Kale-Pea Pod Sauté

Swiss Chard

Beets with Orange Zest

Pickled Vegetables

Sweet 'n Sour Cabbage

Rikke's Sweet Parsnips

Italian-Style Spinach

Autumn Roasted Vegetables

Mock Cucumbers and Cream

Quinoa Pilaf

Basic Brown Rice

Green Rice

Kale-Pea Pod Sauté

2-4 SERVINGS   *Two different shapes make this as eye-appealing as it is tasty.*

1 tablespoon	sesame oil
1 small	onion, sliced
1 cup	pod peas (such as snow peas or sugar snap peas), julienned
8 cups	chopped kale
½ teaspoon	salt
¼ teaspoon	pepper

In a large cast-iron skillet with a lid, heat the oil, add the onion, and cook about 5 minutes. Add the pod peas and kale. Stir, cover, and cook over low heat 3 to 5 minutes more. Season with salt and pepper to taste.

82

Swiss Chard

2-3 SERVINGS

Use grandma's cast-iron skillet when making this to add iron to your meal.

8 cups	Swiss chard, stems and greens (wash well)
2 tablespoons	olive oil
½ tablespoon	minced garlic
splash	tamari
pinch	pepper

Trim the leafy portions of the chard from the stems. Slice the stems thinly and set aside. Coarsely chop the leaves.

In a large cast-iron skillet with a lid, sauté the chard stems in oil, then add the garlic and chopped greens. Cover for 5 minutes. Add the tamari and pepper. Greens cook down a lot, so don't overcook.

Beets with Orange Zest

2-4 SERVINGS   *This is brightly colored and so good for you!*

1½ pounds	beets, peeled, sliced, and cooked
	zest from 1 orange
¼ cup	chopped green onion
2 tablespoons	chopped parsley
2	oranges, peeled, cut into segments or pieces
½ cup	Orange Flair dressing (p. 73)
	salt and pepper to taste
	salad greens for four

In a medium bowl, mix the beets, zest, green onion, parsley, and orange pieces. Toss in enough dressing to coat, and season with salt and pepper to taste. Serve over greens.

Pickled Vegetables

Much different than the store-bought jar; crisp, fresh, and light.

½ cup	apple cider vinegar
2 tablespoons	salt
1 tablespoon	minced garlic
2 teaspoons	turmeric
2 teaspoons	cumin seeds
pinch	cayenne
8 cups	assorted chopped vegetables, such as cauliflower, bell peppers, mushrooms, carrots, zucchini, olives, etc.
1 bunch	chopped dill

In a medium saucepan, combine 4 cups cold water with the first 6 ingredients. Simmer about 5 minutes. Cut the vegetables into different shapes; round, square, julienned, etc. Pour the brine over the vegetables, add the dill, cover, and refrigerate overnight.

Sweet 'n Sour Cabbage

2 SERVINGS

Give your vegetables an Asian flair with this dish.

2 cups	chopped onion
2 tablespoons	toasted sesame oil
4 cups	red cabbage, cored and shredded
½ cup	apple cider
3 tablespoons	umeboshi vinegar
1 tablespoon	caraway seeds (optional)

In a large pot, sauté the onion in oil over medium heat until translucent. Add the cabbage and apple cider, and simmer until the cabbage wilts, about 15 to 20 minutes. Drain the cabbage and onion. Place in a bowl and season with vinegar and caraway seeds, if desired.

Rikke's Sweet Parsnips

4 SERVINGS

This very flavorful healthy dish comes from the kitchen of a dear friend of mine. Parsnips, sometimes called the white gourmet carrot, are a great side dish to accompany a hearty winter meal.

¼ pound	French green beans, cut into 1½-inch pieces
2 tablespoons	olive oil
4 cups	diced onions
1 pound	parsnips, peeled and quartered
1 teaspoon	salt
¼ teaspoon	pepper

Blanch the green beans by plunging them into rapidly boiling water with a pinch of salt for about 30 seconds, then drop them into cold water to stop the cooking process. Drain.

In a medium cast-iron skillet, heat the oil and cook the onions until translucent. Add the parsnips, salt, and pepper. Cook until the parsnips are tender and almost caramelized. Add the green beans and cook 3 to 5 minutes more.

Italian-Style Spinach

2-4 SERVINGS   *Make certain that you don't overcook this very delicate green.*

¼ cup	pine nuts or sunflower seeds
1½ tablespoons	olive oil
1 small	onion, sliced
½ head	garlic, sliced
2 pounds	fresh spinach, stems removed
1 teaspoon	salt
pinch	pepper
⅛ teaspoon	nutmeg

In a dry skillet, toast the pine nuts and set aside. In a large sauté pan, heat the oil and sauté the onion and garlic until translucent. Add the spinach and spices; cover and cook 5 minutes. Sprinkle with pine nuts before serving.

Autumn Roasted Vegetables

12 SERVINGS

Simple, easy, and delicious; toss with a little balsamic vinegar and fresh herbs. Note that some vegetables cook longer than others; it is best to roast each vegetable on its own sheet pan.

½ pound	parsnips, peeled and quartered
½ pound	carrots, peeled and sliced
2 pounds	sweet potatoes, peeled and cubed
2 pounds	onions, chopped
6 to 8 cloves	garlic
2 pounds	white potatoes
splash	olive oil
	salt and pepper to taste
splash	balsamic vinegar
½ cup	chopped fresh parsley

Preheat the oven to 350°F. Lightly toss the vegetables with the olive oil, salt, and pepper, and bake until they are soft yet firm enough so that they will not fall apart. Cool slightly, place in a large bowl, and drizzle with a little olive oil and balsamic vinegar, if desired. Sprinkle with parsley before serving.

Mock Cucumbers and Cream

4 SERVINGS *This creamy sauce is unbelievably delicious.*

1 tablespoon	white miso
2 teaspoons	tahini
¼ cup	rice vinegar
1 tablespoon	mirin
2 to 3 medium	cucumbers, peeled, seeded, and cut in half-circles
½ small	red onion, cut in thin half-circles
pinch	cayenne

Make a paste with the miso, tahini, rice vinegar, and mirin. Stir in the cucumbers, red onion, and cayenne. Serve.

Quinoa Pilaf

4 SERVINGS *Quinoa is one of the oldest known grains and was a staple food of the Aztecs. It cooks like rice in less time and is a rich source of protein.*

1 cup	quinoa
2 cups	water
1 tablespoon	olive oil
⅓ cup	chopped onions or green onions
1 cup	sliced mushrooms
1 small	carrot, grated
½ cup	frozen peas
¼ cup	chopped parsley
	salt and pepper to taste

Rinse the quinoa well in a fine strainer. In a medium pot, bring the water to a boil, and add the quinoa. Cover and simmer 25 to 35 minutes. In a medium skillet, heat the oil and sauté the onions and mushrooms 2 to 3 minutes. Add the carrot and peas. Cover, turn off heat, and let sit until the carrot and peas have been heated through. Stir vegetables into the quinoa. Add the parsley and season to taste.

Variation: Add any vegetables or herbs you wish.

Basic Brown Rice

3-4 SERVINGS *Enhance your rice with flavored oils, salt, gomasio (p. 72), herbs, tamari, or other seasonings.*

1 cup   short-grain rice
2 cups   water

Wash and drain the rice. Cook, covered, in a medium pot of water 40 to 45 minutes over low heat. Keep covered and let stand 5 minutes before serving.

Green Rice

4-6 SERVINGS *This dish combines grains and vegetables with great success.*

1 tablespoon   olive oil
¼ cup   chopped green onions
2 teaspoons   garlic
1 teaspoon   cumin
               salt and pepper to taste

2 cups   chopped fresh spinach
⅓ cup   chopped cilantro
½ cup   chopped parsley
4 cups   hot cooked brown or basmati rice

In a medium pan, heat the oil and sauté the green onions, garlic, cumin, salt, and pepper 3 to 4 minutes. Stir in the spinach, cilantro, and parsley; cover and cook 3 minutes more. Add to the rice, and stir thoroughly.

THE VEGETARIAN Entrées CHICAGO DINER

Scrambled Tofu

Shepherd's Pie

Eggplant Fans

Eggplant Scallopini

Pot Pie

Sloppy Joes

Polenta

Diner Cutlets

Tofu Roulade

Vegetable Paella

Thai Broccoli Tofu Stir-Fry

Tofu Yung

Biryani Stew

Seitan Goulash

Stroganoff

Tofu Spinach Lasagne

Moussaka

No-Meata Fajitas!

Tofu Loaf

Gado Gado

Black Bean-Grain Burgers

Basic Gluten (Seitan)

Lentil Loaf

Ratatouille Provençal

Scrambled Tofu

4 SERVINGS

Scrambled tofu has been a longtime favorite at the Chicago Diner. This recipe gives you the basics. Be creative and spice up your entrée.

1 pound	firm tofu, drained at least 15 minutes
1 tablespoon	sunflower seeds or other nuts
1 tablespoon	sesame seeds or other nuts
1 tablespoon	tamari or soy sauce
1 tablespoon	tahini
⅛ teaspoon	turmeric for color (optional)

Mash the tofu with a potato masher or fork. Mix with all the remaining ingredients until uniformly combined. Sauté the mixture in a lightly oiled skillet 3 to 5 minutes, and turn to brown the other side 3 to 5 minutes more. Just like scrambled eggs, scrambled tofu is very versatile in a number of ways.

Variations:

- To make Italian-style, add garlic, basil, and oregano.

- To make Mexican-style, add cumin, chili powder, and cayenne.

- To make Indian-style, add curry, ginger, and garlic.

- Make a breakfast burrito (p. 32) by adding sautéed onions, broccoli, mushrooms, peppers, cheese, etc. Wrap in a tortilla.

Shepherd's Pie

A hearty comfort food, just as satisfying as the original, but without the meat. Goes great with Diner Gravy (p. 129) on top!

FILLING:

8 ounces	tempeh, cubed
2 tablespoons	olive oil
1 tablespoon	tamari
1 medium	onion, chopped
1 stalk	celery, chopped
½ pound	mushrooms, sliced
3 small	carrots, chopped
1	bay leaf
½ teaspoon	salt
½ teaspoon	sage
½ teaspoon	thyme
½ teaspoon	basil
2 cups	cooked lentils

TOPPING:

3 or 4	potatoes, peeled and boiled until tender
	salt, nutmeg, and pepper to taste
½ to 1 cup	soymilk
1 tablespoon	extra-virgin olive oil

Preheat the oven to 350°F. In a medium saucepan, sauté the tempeh with the oil and tamari until the tempeh starts to brown. Continue sautéing, adding onion, celery, mushrooms, and carrots. Stir in remaining filling ingredients except lentils. When the carrots are tender, add lentils. Stir and simmer until the liquid has evaporated.

In a medium bowl, mash the potatoes with the olive oil and soymilk. Add salt, nutmeg, and pepper to taste. Set aside. Pour the vegetable-lentil mixture into a lightly oiled 10-inch pie pan or 3- to 4-quart casserole, and top with the mashed potatoes. Bake 25 to 30 minutes.

Eggplant Fans

4 SERVINGS

I like to serve the eggplant fans over a bed of spinach pasta and add a little Parmesan to the finished dish.

2	eggplants (about 1 pound each)
6	firm, ripe plum tomatoes
3 pounds	onions, halved and sliced
5 cloves	garlic, coarsely minced
1 cup	marinated artichoke hearts, halved or quartered
1 cup	kalamata olives, pitted
⅓ cup	chopped fresh basil
2 teaspoons	Italian herbs
3	bay leaves
⅓ cup	olive oil
1½ teaspoons	salt
¼ teaspoon	pepper

Preheat the oven to 350°F.

Trim the tops from the eggplants, and cut in half lengthwise. Cut the halves lengthwise at 1-inch intervals, leaving 1½ inches of the top intact. Cut the tomatoes into wedges of irregular widths. Stuff the eggplant slices with overlapping tomato wedges. (Start from the top with the thinner wedges, working down the length of the eggplants.) Place the eggplants in a single layer in a large baking dish. Smother with onions, garlic, artichoke hearts, olives, and herbs. Drizzle with olive oil, salt, and pepper, and cover with foil. Bake 50 to 60 minutes, or until the eggplants are tender and juicy.

Eggplant Scallopini

4 SERVINGS   *For extra excitement, sprinkle a little Parmesan on top!*

4 to 6	heads garlic, coarsely minced
2 pounds	onions, sliced
2 to 3	bay leaves
⅓ cup	olive oil
1 pound	mushrooms, quartered
1 large	eggplant, sliced lengthwise and cut into long strips
2	plum tomatos, cut into wedges
2 teaspoons	salt
½ teaspoon	pepper
1 teaspoon	oregano
1 teaspoon	basil
½ cup	red wine
	parsley for garnish

In a large skillet, sauté the garlic, onions, and bay leaves in the olive oil. Gradually add the mushrooms and eggplant strips. Simmer 10 minutes. Add tomatoes, salt, pepper, herbs, and wine. Simmer 10 minutes more. Season to taste. Serve over pasta or rice, and sprinkle with fresh parsley upon serving.

Pot Pie

6-8 SERVINGS

We once served this pot pie at a wedding for two hundred people. The meat-eaters thought they were eating chicken! You can substitute tofu or tempeh for the seitan if you like.

MARINADE:

¾ cup	water
¾ cup	white wine
1 tablespoon	nutritional yeast
1 tablespoon	onion powder
1 tablespoon	garlic powder
½ teaspoon	dried dill weed
1½ teaspoons	poultry spice, or
	½ teaspoon sage + ½ teaspoon thyme
1 teaspoon	salt
¼ teaspoon	pepper
1 pound	seitan, cubed

VEGETABLES:

1 cup	chopped onion
1 cup	thinly sliced carrot
1 medium	potato, diced
1 cup	chopped celery
½ cup	frozen peas
½ to ⅔ cup	unbleached flour

In a casserole or medium pan, whisk together all the marinade ingredients. Add seitan and marinate 20 to 30 minutes. Drain, reserving the liquid. Bake on an oiled sheet pan 20 to 30 minutes, stirring twice. Set aside.

Preheat the oven to 375°F. To prepare the vegetables, sauté the onion, carrot, and potato until almost soft. Add the celery; cook 5 minutes and add peas. Add ½ to ⅔ cup of unbleached flour to the reserved liquid, and stir well. Pour slowly over the vegetable mixture, then add seitan. Cook until thick, about 5 minutes.

Pour into a 4-quart casserole, top with a prepared pie crust (p. 145), and bake 35 to 40 minutes.

Sloppy Joes

4-5 SERVINGS   *Perfect for afternoon barbeques! Everyone loves our sloppy joes, served on a toasted bun with homestyle potatoes.*

1 pound	tempeh, diced
2 tablespoons	tamari
3 tablespoons	vegetable oil
1½ pounds	onions, diced
2 cloves	garlic, minced
1 pound	bell peppers, diced
1 tablespoon	chili powder
2 tablespoons	oil
1¼ cups	catsup
¼ tablespoon	prepared yellow mustard
1 teaspoon	liquid smoke
½ cup	water
	salt and pepper to taste

Preheat the oven to 350°F. Toss the tempeh in the tamari and oil. Place the tempeh on a sheet pan and bake 15 to 20 minutes, or until golden brown but not crisp. Sauté the onions, garlic, peppers, and chili powder in 2 tablespoons oil. Add the baked tempeh, catsup, mustard, liquid smoke, and a splash of water if needed. Simmer 10 minutes more. Season with salt and pepper. Serve on a toasted kaiser bun or hamburger bun.

Note: Tofu can be used in place of the tempeh. For an even heartier texture, add a little chopped seitan.

Polenta

4 SERVINGS

The sky is the limit with polenta! It can even be used as a crust in many dishes.

1¼ cups	coarse cornmeal
2 teaspoons	salt
¼ teaspoon	pepper
1 teaspoon	garlic powder
4 cups	cold water

OPTIONAL:

	corn kernels
	chopped red bell peppers
	chopped jalapeños
2 teaspoons	nutritional yeast

In a medium saucepan, mix the cornmeal, salt, pepper, and garlic with the cold water, stirring constantly, over medium heat. The mixture will thicken. Test by placing a wooden spoon in the middle of the mixture; when done, your spoon will stand straight up. Add any optional ingredients. Pour the mixture into an oiled pie, loaf, or sheet pan, and chill. After the mixture has settled and chilled, slice or cut it with cookie cutters. To serve, brown the polenta on both sides in a skillet. Top with sautéed vegetables, assorted mushrooms, cheese, marinara sauce, etc.

Diner Cutlets

2-4 SERVINGS *Better known as faux fish fillets. You can use the cutlets as a main course, or put them on a toasted bun for a light sandwich. Great when served with Tartar Sauce (p. 126) or Diner Gravy (p. 129).*

1 pound	tofu, cut into 4 to 6 slabs

MARINADE:

4 to 6 tablespoons	oil
1½ cups	water
1 tablespoon	nutritional yeast
1 teaspoon	salt
½ teaspoon	pepper
1 tablespoon	dried parsley
2 teaspoons	garlic powder
2 teaspoons	onion powder

DRY MIX:

1 cup	cornmeal
½ cup	flour
1 teaspoon	dried parsley
½ teaspoon	salt
½ teaspoon	onion powder
½ teaspoon	garlic powder
½ teaspoon	pepper

Wrap the tofu slabs in plastic wrap and then tin foil. Freeze at least 48 hours. To thaw, remove the wrap and foil. Place the tofu in a dish, and cover with warm water. While the tofu is defrosting, make the marinade.

Mix all the marinade ingredients in a shallow pan. Remove the tofu slices from the water and gently squeeze them with the palm of your hands. They will look spongy. Add the tofu slices to the marinade and let sit for 30 minutes.

Mix the dry ingredients in a shallow baking dish. Remove the tofu slices from the marinade, press out most of the liquid, and coat with the dry mix. Heat the oil in a skillet, and panfry the tofu slices until crispy.

Variation: You can use crumbled seasoned bread crumbs in place of the dry mix.

Tofu Roulade

4-6 SERVINGS

This is also known as the Diner's famous Tofu Turkey. A big thanks to my friend Ron Pickarski for teaching me not only this amazing recipe, but also the joy of cooking healthfully.

CROUTON STUFFING:

½ stick	soy margarine
1 small	onion, diced
1 teaspoon	minced garlic
2 stalks	celery, diced
2 teaspoons	sage
2 teaspoons	thyme
1 teaspoon	salt
½ teaspoon	pepper
5 to 6 cups	croutons
2 tablespoons	chopped parsley
2 to 3 cups	vegetable stock

TOFU ROULADE:

3 pounds	tofu
½ cup	cornstarch
1 tablespoon	agar
1½ teaspoons	salt
¼ teaspoon	pepper
1 tablespoon	parsley
1½ tablespoons	onion powder
1½ tablespoons	garlic powder
3 tablespoons	nutritional yeast

For the stuffing, melt the margarine in a large pot. Add the onions, garlic, celery, and herbs. Cook 5 to 8 minutes over medium heat. Season with salt and pepper. Add the croutons and parsley, and cook 1 to 2 minutes more. Check to see if you need a little more stock or water; the stuffing should be just lightly moistened throughout. Remove from the heat, set aside, and cool.

Note: The key to this recipe is the stuffing needs to be somewhat stiff, not mushy. You can use your favorite stuffing as long as it is tight and solid.

Drain the tofu and mash in a medium bowl with the remaining roulade ingredients. Puree the tofu mixture in a food processor and season to taste. (You may have to do this in 2 batches, depending on the size of your machine.) The purée will be thick. Place a 12- to 14-inch-long sheet of plastic wrap on the table. Pour out the tofu mixture onto the plastic wrap, and pat it down into an oblong shape with a spatula. Place another sheet of wrap the same size as the first sheet over the top of the tofu mixture, and roll smooth with a rolling pin into a 5 x 10-inch rectangle.

Preheat the oven to 350°F. Remove the top piece of plastic. Place cooled stuffing down the middle of the tofu. Fold both sides of the tofu over the middle to cover the stuffing. Twist the ends of the plastic wrap. Wrap the roulade again in foil, twisting the ends. Place the tofu roll on a baking sheet, and bake 1 to 1¼ hours. (The plastic wrap will not melt, and it will help the roulade keep its shape.) Let it set before unwrapping and slicing. Serve with Diner Gravy (p. 129) or Shiitake Mushroom Sauce (p. 130).

Vegetable Paella

6-8 SERVINGS   *This rice stew from Spain is colorful and hearty—a real crowd-pleaser!*

MARINADE:

1 tablespoon	garlic powder
1 tablespoon	onion powder
1 teaspoon	turmeric
3 tablespoons	tamari
2½ cups	water
2 tablespoons	oil

PROTEIN:

1 cup	cubed tempeh
1 cup	cubed tofu
1 cup	cubed seitan

VEGETABLES:

1½ quarts	water
3 ears	fresh or frozen corn
4	carrots
1 small	onion, chopped
3 cloves	garlic, minced
5 tablespoons	olive oil
1 teaspoon	turmeric, or ½ teaspoon saffron
2½ cups	vegetable stock, water, or miso broth
	salt and pepper to taste
½	green bell pepper
½	red bell pepper
1 small	zucchini squash
1 small	yellow squash
2 medium	plum tomatoes, quartered
2 to 3 cups	cooked basmati rice
1 (14.5-ounce) can	diced tomatoes with juice
⅓ cup	chopped parsley
½ cup	green peas (optional)
1 cup	canned artichoke quarters (optional)
	cayenne pepper or hot sauce to taste

Preheat the oven to 350°F. Mix all the marinade ingredients together in a medium bowl. Add the tofu, tempeh, and seitan cubes, toss, and let sit about 20 minutes. Drain off the marinade and bake the cubes on an oiled cookie sheet 15 to 20 minutes. Set aside.

Bring the water to a boil. Add the corn and cook 4 to 5 minutes. Set aside. When cool, slice into 2-inch "wheels." In a large pot over medium-high heat, sauté the carrots, onion, and garlic in olive oil. Cook 5 minutes, and add the turmeric. Continue stirring and add the vegetable broth, salt, and pepper. Cover and cook 3 to 4 minutes. Reduce the heat. Add the bell peppers, squash, baked tofu, tempeh, and seitan, and cook 6 to 8 minutes more. Continue cooking, gradually adding the plum tomatoes and cooked rice. Add the canned tomatoes. Gently stir in the corn, and top off with green peas and artichokes, if desired. Season with cayenne to taste. Serve on a large serving platter, and garnish with parsley.

Thai Broccoli Tofu Stir-Fry

4 SERVINGS *This has been one of the biggest hits since we added it to our menu!*

PEANUT SAUCE:

1 cup	peanut butter
1 cup	hot water
½ cup	apple cider vinegar
1 tablespoon	tamari
1 tablespoon	molasses
+1 teaspoon	
pinch	cayenne

MARINADE:

¼ cup	soybean oil
3 cups	water
¼ cup	turbinado sugar
1½ teaspoons	garlic powder
1½ tablespoons	onion powder
2 teaspoons	curry powder
2 tablespoons	nutritional yeast
1½ teaspoons	salt
1 pound	tofu, cut into 1-inch cubes

For the peanut sauce, mix all the ingredients in a medium bowl, and stir until smooth. Set aside.

For the tofu, preheat the oven to 350°F. Place the marinade ingredients into a medium mixing bowl, and combine well. Add the tofu cubes and let sit at least 30 minutes; drain. Bake the cubes on an oiled baking sheet 35 to 40 minutes, stirring twice. Set aside.

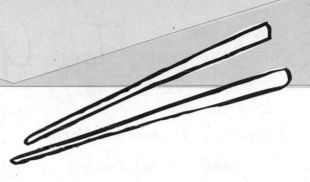

VEGETABLES:

4 cups	broccoli florets
1 medium	onion, sliced
1 clove	garlic, minced
1 medium	red bell pepper, sliced
1 to 3 slices	fresh ginger, julienned
2 tablespoons	peanut oil
	chopped peanuts for garnish

In a medium skillet, sauté the vegetables and ginger in oil. Gradually stir in the marinated tofu cubes. Top with the peanut sauce, and serve over basmati rice. Garnish with chopped peanuts.

Tofu Yung

4 SERVINGS

This Asian vegetable pancake is one of my favorites.

1 pound	firm tofu, well-drained
3 tablespoons	arrowroot or cornstarch
½ teaspoon	ground ginger
1 teaspoon	onion powder
1 teaspoon	salt
¼ teaspoon	pepper
2 tablespoons	chopped parsley
1 teaspoon	turmeric
1 cup	fresh bean sprouts, drained
½ cup	sliced green onions
1 cup	chopped mushrooms
⅓ cup	grated carrots
¼ cup	sesame oil

In a food processor, combine the tofu, arrowroot, ginger, onion powder, salt, pepper, parsley, turmeric, and bean sprouts. Blend until smooth.

Place the tofu mixture in a medium mixing bowl, and add the green onions, mushrooms, carrots, and sesame oil. Blend well. The mixture should be thick. If mixture is too thin, add more drained bean sprouts. Form the mixture into patties, and fry in a skillet until golden brown. Or, bake on an oiled cookie sheet at 350°F for 20 to 30 minutes. The mixture gets firmer when it sets. Serve with rice, snow peas, Soy Ginger Glaze (p. 132) or Diner Gravy (p. 129).

Variation: Substitute shiitake mushrooms, cabbage, peppers, greens, etc., for some of the vegetables.

Biryani Stew

6-8 SERVINGS

Serve this over basmati rice. Dollop with Dairy-Free Sour Cream (p. 126) or yogurt, and garnish with pita triangles.

1 pound	potatoes, diced
2 teaspoons	mustard seeds
¼ cup	oil
2 to 3 medium	onions, diced
2 medium	carrots, diced
3 cups	cauliflower florets
2 medium	bell peppers, assorted colors, sliced
1 small	eggplant, unpeeled, diced
1 to 2 teaspoons	salt
1 teaspoon	cumin
1 teaspoon	coriander
1 teaspoon	turmeric
½ teaspoon	cayenne pepper
2 cups	cooked garbanzo beans (optional)

Parboil the potatoes until cooked but still firm. Set aside.

In a large dry pot, heat the mustard seeds until they begin to toast and pop. Add the oil, onions, carrots, cauliflower, peppers, and eggplant. Cook 8 to 10 minutes. Add the spices, potatoes, and beans, if using. Cover and simmer. You may need to add a little water to the skillet for more moisture.

Variation: Add some sweet potatoes. Parboil separately and add with spices and potatoes.

Seitan Goulash

6 SERVINGS *Our veggie-style goulash with Hungarian paprika is oh-so-good! Serve with a small salad and crispy bread for a hearty lunch.*

MARINADE:

2 tablespoons	vegetable oil
2 teaspoons	onion powder
1 teaspoon	salt
1½ teaspoons	paprika
1 teaspoon	thyme
½ teaspoon	black pepper
1	bay leaf
½ cup	tamari
3 cups	water

SEITAN:

½ pound	seitan, sliced into strips
1½ cups	unbleached all-purpose flour
2 teaspoons	garlic powder
1 teaspoon	onion powder
1 teaspoon	paprika
¼ cup	vegetable oil

VEGETABLES:

2 tablespoons	vegetable oil
2 medium	onions, diced
2 cups	chopped carrots, sliced
3 to 5	potatoes, diced
2	bay leaves
1 cup	chopped celery
1 large	red or green bell pepper, diced

To make the marinade, heat 2 tablespoons oil in a large skillet. Add the remaining marinade ingredients, and simmer 5 to 10 minutes. Remove the bay leaf and discard. Pour marinade over the seitan and let sit for 15 to 25 minutes; drain, reserving the marinade. Mix the flour, garlic powder, onion powder, and paprika in a bowl. Heat the ¼ cup oil in a medium skillet until hot. Dredge the seitan in the flour mixture and sauté until brown. Remove from the skillet and set aside.

Heat the 2 tablespoons oil for the vegetables in a large pot. Add the onions and carrots, and cook 8 to 10 minutes. Add the potatoes and bay leaves, and cook 10 to 15 minutes more, or until the potatoes start to get tender. Add the celery and bell pepper, cover with the reserved marinade, and simmer 5 minutes. Add the seitan, stir, and cover. Season to taste with more paprika. Serve on hot noodles and top with Dairy-Free Sour Cream (p. 126).

Stroganoff

6 SERVINGS   *This is a favorite winter dish.*

MARINADE:

½ cup	white wine
1½ cups	water
1 tablespoon	nutritional yeast
1 teaspoon	garlic powder
1 teaspoon	onion powder
2 teaspoons	paprika
2 teaspoons	thyme
2 teaspoons	salt
1 pound	tofu cubes, tempeh cubes, or seitan strips

SAUCE:

1 large	onion, sliced
2 cloves	garlic, minced
2 tablespoons	vegetable oil
1 pound	mushrooms, sliced
1 small	red bell pepper, sliced in strips
1 cup	water
3 to 4 tablespoons	unbleached flour
1 cup	Dairy-Free Sour Cream (p. 126)
	salt and pepper to taste

Preheat oven to 350°F. Whisk all the marinade ingredients together, and pour over your choice of tofu, tempeh, or seitan. Marinate 20 to 25 minutes. Drain and reserve the liquid. Bake tofu, tempeh, or seitan 20 to 25 minutes on an oiled baking sheet, stirring twice, until browned; set aside.

In a large skillet, sauté the onion and garlic in oil until translucent. Add the mushrooms and pepper, and cook 5 minutes more. Add the water, reserved marinade, and tofu, tempeh, or seitan. Bring to a simmer, and add flour slowly, stirring to prevent lumps. Simmer until the mixture thickens, stirring constantly. Add sour cream, and season with salt and pepper. Serve over noodles or rice.

Tofu Spinach Lasagne

6-8 SERVINGS *A very healthy alternative to cheese lasagne. Half the fat and no cholesterol!*

1 pound	lasagne noodles
2 (10-ounce) packages	chopped frozen spinach, thawed, or 2 pounds fresh spinach, chopped
1 pound	soft tofu, drained
1 pound	firm tofu, drained
½ to ¾ cup	soymilk or water
2 tablespoons	lemon juice
½ teaspoon	onion powder
½ teaspoon	garlic powder
1 tablespoon	minced fresh basil
1 teaspoon	oregano
1 teaspoon	nutmeg
½ teaspoon	fennel seeds (optional)
2 teaspoons	salt
4 to 5 cups	tomato sauce

Preheat the oven to 350°F. Cook the lasagne noodles according to package directions, drain, and set aside. Squeeze any liquid from the frozen spinach until it is completely dry, and set aside. Place all the ingredients except the noodles, spinach, and tomato sauce in a blender, and process until smooth. Combine the spinach with the blended tofu. Cover the bottom of a 9 x 13-inch pan with ½ cup of tomato sauce, and layer the lasagne as follows: tomato sauce, noodles, half the tofu-spinach filling. Continue layering, ending with a layer of noodles and tomato sauce. Bake 30 to 40 minutes.

Suggestions: Top with soy cheese, or reserve some of the tofu filling and dollop on top. Or add chopped, cooked vegetables of your choice to spinach layers.

Moussaka

6 SERVINGS *A typical Greek casserole—with a Chicago Diner twist.*

2 medium	eggplants, sliced
1½ tablespoons	salt
1 cup	soymilk
¾ cup	unbleached flour
¼ cup	cornmeal
1 tablespoon	oregano
½ teaspoon	pepper

Slice the eggplants into 1-inch-thick rounds. Place the rounds in a bowl, cover with water and salt, and soak for 30 minutes. Drain and rinse the rounds, and dry them on paper towels.

Preheat the oven to 350°F. Oil a baking sheet. Pour the soymilk into a medium bowl. In another bowl, mix together the flour, cornmeal, oregano, and pepper. Dip each eggplant slice in the milk, then into the flour mixture. Place the eggplants on an oiled sheet pan, and bake until tender, approximately 30 to 45 minutes. Set aside.

FILLING:			
8 ounces	tempeh, crumbled	1 (16-ounce) can	white beans, drained
2 tablespoons	olive oil	1 or 2	cinnamon sticks
1 tablespoon	tamari	½ teaspoon	salt
1 medium	onion, chopped	¼ teaspoon	pepper
3 to 4 cloves	garlic, minced	2 tablespoons	chopped parsley
2 to 3	plum tomatoes, diced	½ teaspoon	cinnamon

Preheat the oven to 350°F. Mix the crumbled tempeh with 1 tablespoon oil and 1 tablespoon tamari, and bake about 10 minutes.

In a medium pot, heat the remaining tablespoon of oil, add the onion, and cook until translucent. Add the cooked tempeh, garlic, tomatoes, beans, cinnamon sticks, salt, and pepper. Cook 10 minutes more, add parsley and cinnamon; set aside.

BÉCHAMEL SAUCE:

½ cup	oil
½ cup	unbleached flour
4 cups	soymilk or dairy milk
½ teaspoon	salt
pinch	pepper
¼ teaspoon	nutmeg

Heat the oil in a saucepan, and when hot, whisk in the flour. Cook until the nutty smell of the toasting flour comes through. Slowly add the milk, stirring constantly, and cook until thick. Add the salt, pepper, and nutmeg, and set aside.

To assemble the moussaka, place half of the eggplant slices in a single layer in an oiled 13 x 9-inch baking dish. Remove the cinnamon sticks from the filling, and pour in the filling as a second layer. Top with the remaining eggplant slices. Pour the béchamel sauce over the top. Bake 30 to 45 minutes. Let rest for at least 5 minutes before serving.

Note: If using dairy milk in the béchamel sauce, add ⅓ cup of Parmesan cheese, or sprinkle it on top before baking.

No-Meata Fajitas!

4 SERVINGS   *These tempting fajitas will delight even the most dedicated meat eater.*

MARINADE:

½ cup	chopped cilantro
2 to 3	green onions, sliced
½ cup	chopped parsley
1 small	jalapeño pepper, sliced
2 cloves	garlic, chopped
⅓ cup	lemon juice
¼ cup	oil
2 teaspoons	cumin
3 cups	water
2 teaspoons	salt
⅓ cup	tequila (optional)

FAJITA FILLING:

2 tablespoons	oil
1 small	onion, sliced
½ small	red bell pepper, sliced
½ small	green bell pepper, sliced
1 cup	sliced mushrooms
1 medium	tomato, cut in wedges
¼ cup	salsa

1 pound	seitan, cut into lengthwise strips

Mix all the marinade ingredients in a blender. Place the seitan strips in a medium bowl, and pour the marinade over them. Marinate at least 1 hour or overnight.

To prepare the fajita filling, heat the oil in a medium skillet, and sauté the marinated seitan with the onion, peppers, mushrooms, tomato, and salsa. Simmer 8 to 10 minutes. Serve inside folded tortillas, with beans, rice, guacamole, etc. on the side.

Note: To make crispier seitan strips (which most people like), sauté them in your skillet a little longer before adding the vegetables, or after sautéing, finish cooking them on an oiled baking sheet in a 350°F oven for 25 minutes, stirring often.

THE CHICAGO DINER COOKBOOK

Tofu Loaf

6 SERVINGS

The sky is the limit with tofu loaf. You can add any chopped veggies you want—broccoli, cauliflower, red pepper, etc. You can also fold roasted garlic, sesame seeds, walnuts, arame, or corn into the tofu mixture. Be creative!

¼ cup	canola oil
2 pounds	firm tofu, drained
¼ cup	sunflower seeds, lightly toasted
¾ pound	carrots, minced
¾ pound	onions, minced
3 cloves	garlic, minced
2 tablespoons	canola oil
sprig	dill, minced
	salt and pepper to taste

Preheat the oven to 350°F.

In a food processor, blend the ¼ cup oil and tofu until smooth. Pour the blended tofu into a bowl, and fold in the sunflower seeds. Set aside. Sauté the carrots, onions, and garlic in a medium skillet with the 2 tablespoons of oil until tender; drain. Add the sautéed vegetable mixture to the tofu. Blend well and season with the dill, salt, and pepper. Pour into an oiled 4 x 7-inch bread pan, and bake approximately 1 hour.

Gado Gado

In this recipe, a savory combination of spices blends with the vegetables and tempeh to yield a complete and satisfying meal. A perfect stew to warm you up on cold wintry nights.

8 ounces	tempeh
dash	tamari
3 medium	red potatoes, diced
2 medium	sweet potatoes, peeled and diced
¾ cup	peanut butter
1 (14.5-ounce) can	whole tomatoes, drained (reserve the liquid)
1 teaspoon	salt
1 teaspoon	ground cinnamon
½ teaspoon	ground nutmeg
¼ to ½ teaspoon	cayenne
¼ teaspoon	ground fenugreek*
2 tablespoons	soybean oil
splash	tamari

1 medium	yellow onion, sliced
2 medium	carrots, cut in ½-inch rounds
3 cloves	garlic, minced
2 cups	white mushrooms, halved
1 large	green bell pepper, cut into large dice
1 large	yellow bell pepper, cut into large dice
3 medium	tomatoes, cut into wedges
½ cup	vegetable broth
2 to 3 tablespoons	chopped peanuts
1 cup	chopped fresh spinach

Preheat the grill or broiler. Oil grill or baking sheet. Cut the tempeh into 2 thin layers. Then cut each layer into triangles measuring 1 inch on each side. Lay the triangles on the grill or baking sheet, sprinkle with the tamari, and grill or broil on both sides until golden brown; set aside.

Boil potatoes in water to cover over medium-high heat until almost tender. Drain and set aside. In a blender, place the peanut butter, drained tomatoes, salt, cinnamon, nutmeg, cayenne, and fenugreek. Season with a splash of tamari. Blend until smooth and set aside.

Heat the oil in a large sauté pan over medium heat. Add the onion, carrots, and garlic, and cook 2 to 3 minutes. Add the mushrooms and bell peppers, and sauté 3 to 5 minutes more. Add the peanut butter mixture to the mushroom mixture. Bring to a simmer. Add the grilled tempeh, potatoes, and tomato wedges. Simmer until the flavors are well-blended, about 10 to 15 minutes. Add the reserved tomato juice and the vegetable broth for additional liquid. The tomato wedges should retain their shape. Transfer the mixture to a large bowl, sprinkle with the peanuts and spinach, and serve with basmati rice and pita bread.

*Fenugreek is an herb popular in Indian cooking; it has a nutty flavor, like a combination of celery and maple.

Black Bean-Grain Burgers

8 PATTIES   *Complete protein on a bun. Add salsa and avocado for a real treat.*

1 medium	onion, finely chopped
2 stalks	celery, chopped
2 cloves	garlic, minced
⅓ medium	red bell pepper, diced
2 teaspoons	oregano
1 tablespoon	cumin
2 teaspoons	thyme
½ teaspoon	salt
2 teaspoons	pepper
2 tablespoons	oil
2 cups	cooked black beans, lightly mashed
1 cup	cooked brown rice (should be sticky, not dry)
¼ cup	sunflower seeds, chopped and toasted
¼ cup	quick-cooking rolled oats
2 tablespoons	tamari

Sauté the onion, celery, garlic, pepper, and spices in the oil until tender. Pour into a large mixing bowl with the rest of the ingredients. Mix well. The mixture should hold together to form patties.

Preheat the oven to 350°F. Form the mixture into patties, and place on an oiled baking sheet. Bake about 25 to 30 minutes, turning after 15 minutes. Or, panfry the patties in a medium skillet. Serve on your favorite bun with all the fixin's.

Basic Gluten (Seitan)

ABOUT 2 POUNDS COOKED GLUTEN

This is a basic recipe for seitan, also known as wheat meat. It can be used in a wide variety of recipes that call for meat, depending on how you marinate, slice, amd season it. Examples are sliced round and thin for gyros or cut into thick strips for fajitas.

SEITAN:

4 cups	vital gluten flour
¾ cup	whole wheat flour
3 tablespoons	nutritional yeast
2 tablespoons	onion powder
1½ tablespoons	garlic powder
1½ tablespoons	salt
2 tablespoons	Italian, Mexican, or Asian spices
2¼ cups	warm water
¼ cup	tamari

COOKING BROTH:

3 to 4	bay leaves
	pieces of carrot and celery (trimmed ends and tops are also good for this)
3 cloves	garlic, unpeeled

For the seitan, mix the dry ingredients in a large mixing bowl, then add the water and tamari, kneading well to combine. Your mixture should look like dough. Knead about 10 minutes more, or until the dough comes away from the sides of the bowl. Let the dough rest 15 minutes. Cut into 4 pieces.

Fill a large pot with 5 quarts of water. Add bay leaf, carrot, celery, and garlic. Add the 4 gluten pieces to the pot, and boil about 1½ hours. The gluten will triple in size.

When done, the dough will be firm, not sticky. Drain the liquid, discarding the vegetables, and store the seitan covered with cold water and a splash of tamari in a large container in the refrigerator. After the seitan cools, it is ready to be sliced, diced, marinated and cooked for any recipe. Keeps up to two weeks in the refrigerator covered with water.

Lentil Loaf

8 SERVINGS

Filled with healthy grains, beans, and vegetables, this hearty loaf was one of the very first items on our menu, way back when. It's still a favorite with everyone! Try serving this with garlic mashed potatoes and Diner Gravy (p. 129).

BEANS:

4 cups	water
1	bay leaf
2 cups	lentils

In a medium pot, bring the water, bay leaf, and lentils to a boil. Cook on a low simmer until very tender, 35 to 40 minutes. Save 1½ cups broth.

GRAINS:

½ cup	water
½ cup	bulghur

In a second pot, boil the water and add the bulghur. Stir, cover, and remove from heat.

VEGETABLES:

⅓ cup	sesame seeds	2 teaspoons	sage
⅓ cup	sunflower seeds	2 teaspoons	thyme
⅓ cup	walnuts	½ teaspoon	salt
2 cups	finely diced carrots	¼ teaspoon	pepper
2 cups	finely diced onions	1 tablespoon	parsley
⅔ cup	finely diced celery	1 tablespoon	tamari
2 tablespoons	oil	2 cups	quick-cooking oats

Preheat the oven to 300°F. On a sheet pan, toast the seeds and nuts until they become aromatic; set aside. Increase oven temperature to 350°F. In a large skillet, sauté the vegetables in the oil until soft. Add the herbs, except the parsley, and cook 10 to 12 minutes. Stir in the parsley and tamari. Add the toasted seeds and nuts, lentils, bulghur, and oats, and stir well. The final mixture may need 1 to 1½ cups of the saved lentil broth for more moisture if it is too dry to hold together. Season to taste. Place the loaf in an oiled 4 x 7-inch bread pan, and bake uncovered for 45 minutes. Cover with aluminum foil and bake another 20 to 25 minutes.

Ratatouille Provençal

4-5 SERVINGS   *A delicious use of eggplant and zucchini.*

2 tablespoons	olive oil
1 large	onion, diced
1	bay leaf
2 teaspoons	basil
2 teaspoons	marjoram
2 teaspoons	oregano
4 to 6 cloves	garlic, coarsely cut
1 small	red bell pepper, chopped
1 small	green bell pepper, chopped
1 small	eggplant, cubed
1 medium	zucchini, cut in half-moons

1 small	plum tomato, cut in wedges
10 to 12	kalamata olives, pitted, cut in half
4 to 5 tablespoons	tomato paste
⅓ cup	red wine (optional)
2 teaspoons	salt
½ teaspoon	pepper
dash	tamari
	fresh basil, chopped, for garnish

Heat the oil in a large sauté pan, and sauté the onion until transparent. Add the herbs, peppers, and eggplant. Cover the pan and simmer about 5 minutes. Add the zucchini, tomato, olives, and tomato paste, along with the wine and a little water if necessary to keep the mixture from sticking to the bottom of the pan. Cover and cook 8 minutes more. Season with salt, pepper, and tamari, and pour the mixture into a large bowl. Garnish with fresh chopped basil, and serve with pasta or rice.

Sauces

THE VEGETARIAN CHICAGO DINER

Dairy-Free Sour Cream

Tartar Sauce

Tomato Sauce

White Miso Sauce

Golden Mustard Dill Sauce

Diner Gravy

Shiitake Mushroom Sauce

Sweet Red Pepper Sauce

Korean Red Pepper Sauce

Soy Ginger Glaze

Bolognese Sauce

Alfredo (John) Astin Style

Cheese Sauce

Dairy-Free Sour Cream

1 CUP   *We top off our stroganoff with this sour cream. It tastes great and it's healthful too!*

½ pound	soft tofu
1 tablespoon	soybean oil
2 tablespoons	lemon juice
1 teaspoon	salt

Put all the ingredients into a blender, and process until creamy. Serve well chilled.

Tartar Sauce

1 1/2 CUPS   *At the Chicago Diner, we use this sauce to accompany our filet sandwich.*

1 cup	eggless mayonnaise
⅓ cup	chopped dill pickle
1 tablespoon	lemon juice
	salt and pepper to taste

Mix all the ingredients until creamy.

Tomato Sauce

Always fills the kitchen with a wonderful aroma—Mama Mia!

¼ cup	olive oil
1½ cups	diced onion
1	bay leaf
1 cup	minced bell pepper
3 cloves	garlic, minced
5 to 8	fresh tomatoes, chopped
1 (6-ounce) can	tomato paste
1 (28-ounce) can	crushed tomatoes
1½ teaspoons	oregano
1 teaspoon	basil
½ teaspoon	thyme
1 whole	carrot
	salt and pepper to taste

Heat the oil in a large pot. Add the onion and sauté
5 to 6 minutes. Add bay leaf, bell pepper, and garlic,
and cook 5 minutes more. Add the tomatoes, tomato paste,
crushed tomatoes, herbs, and whole carrot. (The carrot cuts the acidity
from the tomatoes and sweetens the sauce. Remove before serving sauce.)
Simmer 45 minutes. Season with salt and pepper to taste.

Variation: Add ½ cup of red wine 15 minutes before the sauce is done.

White Miso Sauce

ABOUT 2 1/2 CUPS

This creamy white sauce goes well with tofu loaf, veggies, and grains.

2 cups	plain soymilk
¼ cup	white miso
2 tablespoons	mirin
¼ cup	arrowroot or cornstarch mixed with enough cold water to make a thin paste
	salt and pepper to taste
	dill and parsley to taste

In a small saucepan, heat the soymilk over low heat. (Soymilk curdles easily; do not boil.) Whisk in the miso and mirin, and stir until dissolved. To thicken, stir in arrowroot. Season with salt, pepper, dill, and parsley.

Golden Mustard Dill Sauce

ABOUT 1 1/2 CUPS

Tastes great as a dip, or serve it with quiche, or use as a sandwich spread.

1 cup	eggless mayonnaise
¼ cup	yellow mustard
pinch	salt
⅛ teaspoon	black pepper
1 tablespoon	chopped fresh dill

Mix all the ingredients until creamy.

Diner Gravy

8-10 SERVINGS   *Our version of a basic, tasty all-American gravy.*

There are three parts to this recipe: the dry spice mix, the roux, and the base. Any of the parts can be stored and used separately in other dishes. For example, it's nice to keep a jar of this dry mix on hand to add to soups and sauces. You can also make extra roux. It keeps in the refrigerator for a week, and it's great for thickening soups, sauces, and stews.

SPICE MIX:

2½ cups	nutritional yeast	2½ tablespoons	celery seed
⅓ cup	dried parsley	2½ tablespoons	onion powder
1½ tablespoons	salt	2 teaspoons each	basil, oregano, and thyme
1½ tablespoons	dried dill weed	1 teaspoon	rosemary

In a small dry bowl, mix all the ingredients well; store in a dry container.

ROUX:

⅓ cup	soybean oil
⅓ cup	unbleached flour

Heat the oil in a small saucepan. When hot, gently whisk in the flour, stirring constantly, until the flour develops a nutty aroma. (Be careful; it burns easily.) Set aside.

BASE:

4 cups	water or light vegetable stock
⅓ cup	tamari
¼ cup	spice mix

In a medium pot, bring all the base ingredients to a high simmer. Gradually whisk in the roux and cook to desired thickness. Add a little freshly ground pepper to taste. Leftover gravy can be frozen.

Shiitake Mushroom Sauce

6-8 SERVINGS   *Rich and delicious with tasty morsels of mushrooms.*

4 cups	water
1 to 2	bay leaves
2 to 3 cloves	garlic
pinch	black peppercorns, or to taste
1 cup	mushroom stems from shiitakes and/or other mushrooms
3 tablespoons	oil
3 tablespoons	unbleached flour
¼ cup	tamari
½ teaspoon	nutmeg
2 cups	sliced fresh shiitake mushrooms

In a large pot, bring the water to a boil with the bay leaves, garlic, black peppercorns, and mushroom stems. Reduce the heat and simmer 20 minutes. Strain, discarding solids, and return the liquid to the pot. In another small saucepan, make a roux by combining the oil and flour, and cook over medium heat, stirring constantly, until it develops a nutty aroma. Set aside.

Add the tamari, nutmeg, and sliced mushrooms to the strained broth, and bring to a boil. Gradually add the roux a little at a time until the gravy is the desired thickness.

Optional: Use arrowroot or cornstarch to thicken the sauce if you want less fat.

Sweet Red Pepper Sauce

2 CUPS

We serve this sauce with our dairy-free quiche. It also tastes great with polenta, or as a dipping sauce for grilled vegetables.

4 to 5	red bell peppers
1 tablespoon	olive oil
4 to 6 cloves	garlic
⅓ to ½ cup	olive oil
1 teaspoon	salt
¼ teaspoon	pepper

Preheat the oven to 350°F.

Brush the peppers with 1 tablespoon olive oil. Bake on a cookie sheet until browned, about 15 to 20 minutes. Brush the garlic cloves with oil, and add them to the baking sheet during the last 10 minutes. Cool peppers and garlic. Peel the peppers, remove the seeds, and combine them in a blender with the garlic, olive oil, salt, and pepper. Blend until smooth.

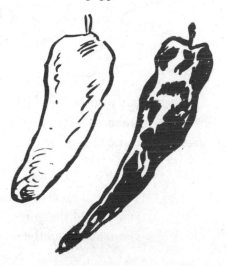

Korean Red Pepper Sauce

ABOUT 3 CUPS

This sauce is a hit on any Asian stir-fry or with anyone wanting to add a kick to their meals!

1½ cups	water
¼ cup	tamari or soy sauce
1 teaspoon	sesame oil
1 teaspoon	grated fresh ginger
1 teaspoon	minced garlic
1 tablespoon	Korean red pepper spice or ½ teaspoon dried red pepper flakes

½ cup	barley malt or other sweetener
½ cup	catsup
¼ cup	mirin
2 to 4 tablespoons	arrowroot or cornstarch

Mix all the ingredients in a medium pot with a whisk, and heat until thickened, stirring occasionally.

Soy Ginger Glaze

2 1/2 CUPS

2 cups	cold water or cold vegetable stock
3 tablespoons	arrowroot or cornstarch
1 tablespoon	grated fresh ginger

¼ cup	tamari
2 tablespoons	mirin

In a small saucepan, mix the water or stock with the arrowroot or cornstarch. Add the ginger, tamari, and mirin. Cook over low heat, stirring constantly, until the mixture thickens.

Bolognese Sauce

6 SERVINGS   *A chunky tomato sauce. Tempeh makes this sauce seem very meaty. Tastes great over pasta.*

8 ounces	tempeh, crumbled
1 tablespoon	olive oil
1 tablespoon	tamari
¼ cup	olive oil
1 cup	chopped onion
2 cloves	garlic, minced
1 cup	chopped bell peppers
1 cup	sliced mushrooms
2 (28-ounce) cans	tomatoes, whole or crushed
1 (6-ounce) can	tomato paste
1 teaspoon	dried basil
1 teaspoon	dried oregano
	salt and pepper to taste
1 (8-ounce) can	artichoke hearts, rinsed and quartered

Marinate the tempeh in 1 tablespoon oil and tamari for 1 hour. Preheat the oven to 350°F. Place the marinated tempeh on a cookie sheet, and bake 10 to 15 minutes. Set aside. In a large saucepan, heat ¼ cup olive oil, and sauté the onion, garlic, peppers, and mushrooms 5 to 8 minutes. Add the tomatoes, tomato paste, herbs, salt and pepper, artichokes, and tempeh. Simmer 45 minutes.

Alfredo (John) Astin Style

ABOUT 3 CUPS

Serve this classic sauce over green spinach pasta with sautéed broccoli, sun-dried tomatoes, red onions, and a sprinkle of pine nuts.

12 ounces	soft tofu, drained	2½ tablespoons	white miso
1 cup	plain yogurt	½ teaspoon	nutmeg
2 tablespoons	lemon juice	1 cup	Parmesan cheese (optional)
2½ tablespoons	tahini		salt and pepper to taste

Blend all the ingredients together in a food processor or blender. Adjust seasonings to taste. Heat and serve. (If it gets too thick, add a little soymilk.)

Cheese Sauce

6-8 SERVINGS

This tastes great served over Ex-Benedict or Eggs Florentine (p. 31).

2 tablespoons	margarine	¼ teaspoon	paprika
2 tablespoons	oil	¼ teaspoon	mustard powder
4 cups	milk	⅛ teaspoon	cayenne pepper
3 to 4 tablespoons	unbleached flour	⅛ teaspoon	white pepper
½ teaspoon	salt	1½ cups	grated white Cheddar cheese

In a small pot, melt the margarine and oil. When hot, whisk in the flour to make a roux, stirring constantly to prevent burning. Continue cooking until flour develops a nutty aroma; set aside.

In a medium pot, heat the milk over low heat. When the milk is hot, add everything except the cheese. Cook the sauce, whisking constantly, until thickened to desired consistency. Add the grated cheese and stir until melted and smooth.

Desserts

THE VEGETARIAN · CHICAGO DINER

Chocolate Mousse

Kanten

Vanilla Cream Custard

Applesauce

Cocoa Oat Bars

Chocolate-Nut Brownies

Oatmeal Raisin Cookies

Chocolate Chipper
Cookies

Thumbprints or Jewels

Basic Pie Crust

Streusel Topping

Apple Pie

Gingerbread Cake

Cocoa Cake

Yellow Lemon Cake

Cheesecake

Chocolate Ganache

German Cake Topping

Maple Cream Whip

Chocolate Icing

Grandma's Fluffy
White Icing

Chocolate Mousse

5-6 SERVINGS

This mousse has many uses, including cake filling or frosting. Serve it alone in a parfait glass, or pour it into a crust for a simple tart.

4 cups	semisweet chocolate chips
2 cups	soymilk
2 tablespoons	maple syrup
12 ounces	firm tofu, drained
1 teaspoon	orange or mint extract (optional)

Melt chocolate chips in the top of a double boiler. Mix the soymilk, sweetener, and tofu in a blender. Add the melted chips and orange extract, blend, and chill. It will firm up as it chills.

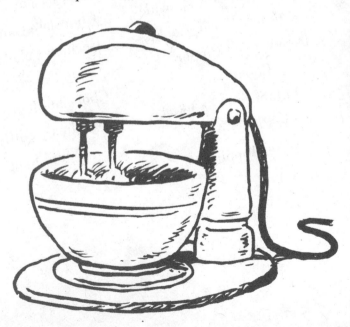

Kanten

This is light and so good to serve after a heavy meal.

4 cups	fruit juice (apple, peach, or strawberry)
4 tablespoons	agar flakes
pinch	salt
1 tablespoon	lemon juice
1 pint	chopped fresh fruit (your choice)
1 to 2 tablespoons	arrowroot mixed with a little water

Bring the juice, agar flakes, salt, and lemon juice to a boil, Reduce the heat and simmer until the agar flakes dissolve. Stir in the chopped raw fruit and the arrowroot mixture.

Pour the mixture into a mold or individual serving dishes; it sets as it chills.

Vanilla Cream Custard

4 SERVINGS   *Great as a cake filling or on its own in parfait glasses.*

2 cups	soymilk
pinch	salt
¾ cup	turbinado sugar
⅓ cup	unbleached flour
2 teaspoons	vanilla extract

In a medium saucepan, heat the soymilk, salt, and sugar. Add the flour, stirring well. As the custard thickens, stir occasionally. Add the vanilla extract. Pour into a prebaked 9-inch pie shell or parfait glasses, and top with fruit. Chill.

Optional: Use arrowroot or cornstarch to thicken the sauce if you want less fat.

Applesauce

ABOUT 6 CUPS

Not only is this a nice way to serve a light dessert, it goes great as a side dish for casseroles and hearty winter entrées. During the fall season, there are as many varieties of apples as there are days. When making apple-sauce, choose an apple that is very tart and suited for baking. Do not use Red or Golden Delicious varieties for applesauce.

3 pounds	apples
¼ cup	lemon juice
½ cup	sweetener (honey, maple syrup, or raw sugar)
pinch	salt
pinch	cinnamon
pinch	nutmeg

Wash and core the apples. Cut them into thin pieces with or without the skins on. (Of course, they will be more nutritious with the skins left on.) Place them in a saucepan with the lemon juice, sweetener, and salt. Cook uncovered 15 minutes until tender. Add cinnamon and nutmeg to taste. The apples can be puréed, mashed, or left chunky. Serve hot or cold. Applesauce freezes well.

Note: Applesauce makes a great substitute for eggs in baking recipes.

Cocoa Oat Bars

12-16 BARS

Some of our favorite guests have had us mail these bars to their family and friends. Make them once, and the aroma alone will win you over.

BOTTOM CRUST:

4 cups	quick-cooking rolled oats
½ cup	maple syrup
pinch	salt
½ cup	hot water

TOPPING:

2 cups	chocolate chips
1 cup	finely chopped walnuts
½ cup	maple syrup
2 cups	shredded coconut
1½ teaspoons	arrowroot or cornstarch

Preheat the oven to 350°F. In a small bowl, mix the oats, maple syrup, salt, and water. Press the mixture evenly into an oiled 9 x 13-inch baking sheet. Or, place plastic wrap on top of the mixture, roll it with a rolling pin, and remove the wrap. Bake 8 to 10 minutes; set aside.

In a medium bowl, combine all the topping ingredients. Pulse this mixture in two batches in a food processor until sticky. Place the topping over the oat crust; using another sheet of plastic wrap, cover the topping and evenly roll out the mixture. Remove the wrap and bake 20 to 25 minutes. Cut while warm. These are best served at room temperature or warm. They can be frozen if you do not want to serve them for a few days.

Chocolate–Nut Brownies

12-16 *Drizzle a little Chocolate Ganache (p. 132) on top of your warm brownies and serve with a scoop of your favorite frozen treat.*

DRY INGREDIENTS:

2½ cups	turbinado sugar
1⅓ cups	unbleached flour
1⅓ cups	whole wheat pastry flour
1⅓ cups	cocoa
2 tablespoons	egg replacer (see p. 155)
2 teaspoons	salt
2 teaspoons	baking powder
1 cup	walnuts

WET INGREDIENTS:

6 ounces	soft tofu
½ cup	soybean oil
1 cup + 1 tablespoon	water
1½ tablespoons	vanilla

Preheat the oven to 350°F. In a medium bowl, sift together the dry ingredients except the walnuts. Mix all the wet ingredients in a blender. Add them to the dry ingredients, and fold in the walnuts. The batter will be thick. Pour into an oiled 9 x 13-inch baking pan, and bake 35 to 40 minutes or until a toothpick inserted in the center comes out clean.

Oatmeal Raisin Cookies

ABOUT 24-36   *Just can't keep them in the cookie jar long enough!*

¾ cup	soy margarine
¼ cup	maple syrup
¾ cup	turbinado sugar
2 teaspoons	vanilla
1½ cups	unbleached flour, or 1 cup unbleached flour + ½ cup whole wheat pastry flour
½ teaspoon	salt
½ teaspoon	cinnamon
1 teaspoon	baking soda
1½ cups	quick-cooking rolled oats
½ cup	raisins
½ cup	nuts and/or chocolate chips (optional)

Preheat the oven to 350°F. Cream together the margarine, maple syrup, sugar, and vanilla. Mix the flour, salt, cinnamon, baking soda, and oats together well with a whisk to combine completely. Combine with the wet ingredients. Fold in the raisins, nuts, and chocolate chips, if using. Oil a cookie sheet or line with parchment paper. Form the dough into cookies, and place on the cookie sheet. Bake 13 to 15 minutes.

Chocolate Chipper Cookies

ABOUT 36   *A big thanks to a dear Diner guest for sharing this recipe with us.*

3 cups	mixture of unbleached and pastry flour
1 teaspoon	baking soda
½ teaspoon	salt
1 cup	soy margarine
¾ cup	maple syrup
1 teaspoon	vanilla extract
⅓ cup	sesame tahini
⅔ cup	semisweet chocolate chips
⅔ cup	walnuts or pecans

Preheat the oven to 350°F. Sift together the flour, baking soda, and salt. Cream the margarine, maple syrup, vanilla extract, and tahini, and stir into the dry ingredients. Fold in the chocolate chips and nuts. Spoon out onto oiled sheet pans, and bake approximately 15 to 18 minutes.

Thumbprints or Jewels

2-3 DOZEN *A nutty treat—it's more than just a cookie. Try these with different nuts and jams.*

1 cup	soy margarine or butter
½ cup	sweetener (honey, maple syrup, rice syrup, or raw sugar)
1 teaspoon	vanilla extract
1 cup	unbleached flour
1¼ cups	pastry flour
½ teaspoon	salt
1 teaspoon	cinnamon
1 cup	chopped or crushed walnuts (or pecans or hazelnuts)
	jellies, jams, or preserves for filling the cookies

Preheat the oven to 350°F. Cream together the margarine, sweetener, and vanilla extract. Sift together the flours, salt, and cinnamon. Fold into the creamed mixture along with the nuts.

Make the dough into 1½-inch balls. Press in the center with your thumb, and fill with your choice of jelly, jam, or preserves. Bake on an oiled cookie sheet 15 to 22 minutes.

Basic Pie Crust

2 CRUSTS   *This simple, easy recipe can be used for fruit or vegetable pies.*

1 cup	unbleached flour
1 cup	whole wheat pastry flour
1 teaspoon	salt
1 teaspoon	baking powder
⅔ cup	soy margarine
¼ to ⅓ cup	ice water

In a medium bowl, stir the dry ingredients with a pastry cutter or fork. Cut in the margarine until the dough is crumbly and pebble-like. Make a well in the center of the bowl, and add the ice water. Mix until the dough forms a ball. You may need to drizzle a little more water to get it to the point where it will hold together. Shape into a ball and divide in half.

Roll out the dough ⅛ inch thick on a floured board or countertop.

Streusel Topping

1 1/2 CUPS   *A quick mix for coffee cakes, muffins, quick breads, and baked fruit.*

¼ cup	turbinado sugar
½ cup	flour, or ¼ cup rolled oats mixed with ¼ cup flour or crushed granola
½ teaspoon	nutmeg
½ teaspoon	cinnamon
½ cup	nuts (optional)
¼ cup	soy margarine

Mix all the ingredients in a bowl and cut in margarine with a fork. Sprinkle on your favorite dessert before baking to add a sweet crunch!

146

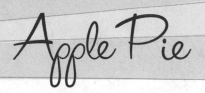

Apple Pie

6-8 SERVINGS   *This great American favorite is simple to make.*

FILLING:

6 cups	sliced apples
1 cup	sweetener
2 tablespoons	flour or 1 tablespoon arrowroot
pinch	salt
1 teaspoon	cinnamon
½ teaspoon	nutmeg
½ tablespoon	lemon juice (from ¼ lemon)
¼ cup	raisins or currants and nuts (optional)
1	unbaked pie shell

Combine all the filling ingredients in a pot, and cook over medium heat just until it starts to thicken.

Preheat the oven to 375°F. Pour the cooked filling into an unbaked pie shell. Add a top layer of crust, or you can make our streusel topping (p. 146). Bake 8 minutes, then reduce the oven temperature to 325°F and bake 40 minutes longer.

Gingerbread Cake

1 LOAF *Moist and delicious with plump raisins and just the right spice!*

½ cup	soymilk
½ tablespoon	white vinegar
½ cup	molasses
¼ cup	maple syrup
¼ cup	soybean oil
2 tablespoons	puréed soft tofu, or 1 tablespoon egg replacer
2 cups	mixture of unbleached and whole wheat pastry flour
¾ teaspoon	baking soda
½ teaspoon	salt
1 tablespoon	ground ginger
½ teaspoon	cinnamon
½ teaspoon	nutmeg
¼ teaspoon	cloves
pinch	cardamom
	zest of ¼ orange
½ cup	raisins

Preheat the oven to 350°F. Mix the liquids in a blender with the tofu. Sift together the remaining ingredients, except the zest and raisins. Mix the wet ingredients with the dry ingredients, and add the zest and the raisins. The batter will be thick. Pour into an oiled loaf pan, and bake 45 to 50 minutes.

Cocoa Cake

When frosted with our vegan Chocolate Mousse, this is one of our most popular cakes at the Chicago Diner!

DRY INGREDIENTS:

1¼ cups	unbleached flour
1 cup	whole wheat pastry flour
½ cup	cocoa
½ teaspoon	salt
¾ teaspoon	baking soda
¾ teaspoon	baking powder

WET INGREDIENTS:

1¾ cups	maple syrup
1 cup	water
5 tablespoons	oil or melted soy margarine
1 teaspoon	vanilla extract
1 teaspoon	white vinegar

Preheat oven to 350°F. Oil an 8-inch cake pan or cupcake tins. Sift the dry ingredients together. In a separate bowl, whisk together the wet ingredients. Mix the dry ingredients into the wet ingredients gradually, until smooth. Pour the batter into prepared pan or cupcake tins, and bake 30 to 35 minutes until a toothpick inserted in the center comes out clean.

Yellow Lemon Cake

8 SERVINGS

To make this a vanilla cake, use 1¼ cups vanilla soymilk instead of lemon juice, replace the lemon extract with vanilla extract, and use no lemon zest.

DRY INGREDIENTS:

2 cups	unbleached flour
2 cups	whole wheat pastry flour
2 teaspoons	baking soda
2 teaspoons	baking powder
1 teaspoon	salt

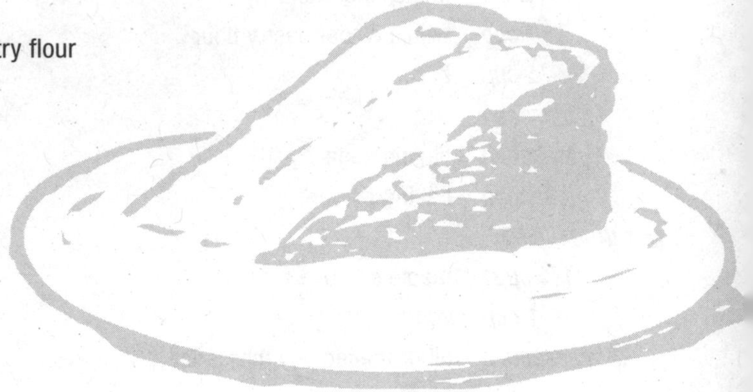

WET INGREDIENTS:

½ cup	lemon juice
¾ cup	soybean oil
¾ cup	soymilk
1¾ cups	maple syrup
1 teaspoon	lemon extract
	zest of ½ lemon
2 teaspoons	white vinegar

Preheat the oven to 350°F. Mix the dry ingredients in a medium bowl. Mix the wet ingredients in another medium bowl. Combine the wet ingredients with the dry ingredients, and mix until smooth. Pour into an oiled 8- or 9-inch round pan. Bake 1 hour or until a toothpick inserted in center comes out clean.

Cheesecake

This creamy sweet "cheese" cake will tempt even the most discerning cheesecake lover! Dairy-free and delicious, it has been a longtime favorite among our guests at the Chicago Diner. You can top with ganache or fresh fruit.

CRUST:

1¾ cups	granola*, graham cracker crumbs, or cookie crumbs
2 tablespoons	soy margarine, melted
1 tablespoon	water

*We use a wheat-free granola. It's another nice option to offer your wheat-allergy friends.

FILLING:

2 pounds	soft tofu
2½ tablespoons	lemon juice
¾ cup	maple syrup, honey, or granulated sugar
⅓ cup	canola or light vegetable oil
1 tablespoon	vanilla extract
2 teaspoons	lemon zest
1 cup	chocolate chips, chopped fruit, or coconut (optional)

Preheat the oven to 350°F.

Break up the granola in a blender or food processor. Mix in the melted margarine and water. If it is still very crumbly, add an additional tablespoon of water. Press the mixture firmly into an 8-inch springform pan or 10-inch pie pan, and bake 8 to 10 minutes.

Place all the filling ingredients except optional ingredients in a blender or food processor, and process until smooth. Fold optional ingredients into the mixture. Pour the filling into the crust, and bake 25 to 35 minutes. The top of the cheesecake should spring back at a light touch. The cheesecake becomes firmer as it cools. Cool completely before slicing.

Chocolate Ganache

ABOUT 2 CUPS *Great as a sauce for dipping or coating.*

1½ cups	soymilk
1 tablespoon	soy margarine
24 ounces	semisweet chocolate chips (3½ to 4 cups)
1 tablespoon	orange or raspberry liqueur (optional)

In a small saucepan, heat the soymilk and margarine. Stir the chocolate chips into the warm soymilk mixture, and mix well until the chocolate is melted and the mixture is smooth. Add liqueur, if desired. The ganache is ready to use now as a sauce, or chill it in the refrigerator to frost cakes.

German Cake Topping

ABOUT 3 CUPS *Gooey-rich, sweet, and nutty; you can serve this over ice cream too.*

¼ cup	soy margarine
½ cup	raw sugar
½ cup	barley malt
1 cup	coconut
⅔ cup	chopped walnuts or pecans
1 teaspoon	vanilla extract

Place the margarine, sugar, and barley malt in a saucepan, and melt. Simmer 2 minutes and remove from the heat. Add the remaining ingredients, and stir well.

Maple Cream Whip

1 1/2 CUPS

This easy-to-make whipped cream tastes great on your homemade pies, brownies, fresh fruit, and even hot cocoa!

8 ounces	soft silken tofu, drained
2 teaspoons	soybean or safflower oil
⅓ cup	maple syrup
pinch	salt
1 teaspoon	vanilla extract

Purée all the ingredients in a blender. Serve well chilled.

Chocolate Icing

1 1/2 CUPS

This starts out very thin. Cool until firm and then beat until fluffy.

8 ounces	semisweet chocolate chips, melted (1¼ cups)
1 cup	soy margarine
½ cup	rice syrup or honey
1 teaspoon	vanilla extract
1 cup	soft tofu, drained

Melt the chocolate chips. Cream the soy margarine with the rice syrup and vanilla. Blend the tofu, and add to the creamed mixture. Add the melted chocolate chips and stir well. Chill. Beat 5 minutes before frosting.

Tip: Melt chocolate chips in the top of a double boiler.

Grandma's Fluffy White Icing

ABOUT 4 CUPS

It's light, fluffy, and not too sweet. Thanks, Gram!

2 cups	soymilk
1¼ cups	unbleached flour
2 cups	soy margarine
1¼ cups	raw sugar or honey
2 teaspoons	vanilla extract
1 teaspoon	agar powder

In a small saucepan, heat the soymilk with the flour, and cook until thick and pasty, stirring constantly to avoid burning. Remove from the heat and put into a bowl. Cover with plastic wrap and cool. In a mixer, cream the margarine and sugar until light and fluffy. Add the cooled flour paste, vanilla extract, and agar. Blend on high speed until light and fluffy.

154

Glossary

AGAR: Also called agar agar. An odorless, tasteless gelling agent made from sea vegetables. Available in powder and flakes.

ARAME: A thick, black sea vegetable with a mild flavor. Available at natural food stores and Asian markets.

ARROWROOT POWDER: A starchy powder made from the root of a tropical plant. Used for thickening. Less processed than cornstarch, but can be substituted for cornstarch measure for measure. Available at natural food stores and most supermarkets.

BALSAMIC VINEGAR: Made from grapes and aged in barrels. Has a sweet/sour flavor. Available in most supermarkets.

BARLEY MALT: Barley that has been sprouted, dried, and ground into a powder. Has a mellow, slightly sweet flavor. Available in natural food stores.

EGG REPLACER: A powdered starch that can be used in baked goods as an egg replacer. Sold in natural food stores.

GLUTEN FLOUR: Flour that has been treated to remove most of the starch, making it high in gluten, a grain protein that gives dough its elasticity. Available in most supermarkets and natural food stores (may be called "bread flour").

GOMASIO: A seasoning blend of ground sesame seeds and salt. Available in natural food stores.

KELP: See "kombu."

KOMBU: A thick, dark green sea algae, used to flavor slow-cooking soups, stews, and bean dishes, and in sushi and other dishes. Available in strips and as a powder in natural food stores and Japanese markets. Also called "kelp."

MIRIN: Japanese cooking wine made from sweet brown rice.

MISO: A salty paste made from cooked soybeans and sometimes grains. Varieties range from light with a mellow flavor to dark, stronger flavors. Available in Asian and natural food stores.

NUTRITIONAL YEAST: Yeast that is grown on molasses and has a mellow, rich flavor. Available in yellow flakes or powder at natural food stores.

QUINOA: A round, sand-colored grain with a nutty taste and light, fluffy texture.

RAW SUGAR: The food that is left after sugar cane has been processed to remove the molasses. Flavor is similar to brown sugar.

RICE VINEGAR: A Japanese vinegar made from fermented rice. Available in Asian markets, natural food stores, and most supermarkets.

SEITAN: A meat substitute made from boiled wheat gluten. It can be purchased prepared, frozen, or as a quick mix. Available in natural food stores.

SOBA: Flat, grayish brown Japanese noodles made from buckwheat and yam.

TAHINI: A thick, smooth paste made from ground sesame seeds. Available in many supermarkets and Middle Eastern groceries.

TAMARI: Dark, fermented soy sauce made without sugar, a byproduct of making miso. Available in most supermarkets.

TEMPEH: A food made from fermented soybeans and sometimes grains. It has a chewy, "meaty" texture and a nutty taste, and can be used in recipes as a meat substitute. Available in natural food stores.

TURBINADO SUGAR: Raw sugar that has been steam-cleaned. It is golden in color and has a light molasses flavor.

UDON NOODLES: Thick Japanese noodles made from wheat or corn.

UMEBOSHI VINEGAR: A vinegar made from Japanese plums. Available in Asian markets and in some natural food stores.

Index